THE HANDBOOK OF

GW00659643

BRITISH RAILWAYS

STEAM MOTIVE
POWER DEPOTS

CONTENTS

VOLUME THREE
NORTH MIDLANDS
LANCASHIRE & YORKSHIRE
PAUL SMITH

PLATFORM
5

This book is dedicated to

MOM and DAD

Ex-LMS Class 5 4–6–0 No. 45212 of Lostock Hall MPD on one of the last ever duties by a steam locomotive on BR. It was photographed at Preston Station on August 4th, 1968 whilst supplying steam heat to a rake of sleeping cars. Upon completing the task it returned to its depot where it was officially withdrawn from service and the shed closed.   *CA Hibbert*

ACKNOWLEDGEMENTS

Once again may I offer my sincere thanks to those people, without whose help and guidance this work would not have been possible. I would particularly like to acknowledge, for their contributions to this particular volume:

Chris Bush, Roger Griffiths, Nick Pigott, Philip Stuart, Stan Robinson. JW Henshaw and Tony Foster of the Engine Shed Society.

Peter Rowbotham, Ken Plant and Les Nixon, and Charlie Herring of Stanton PLC for their help in sorting out sub-sheds in Derbyshire.

Mr R.Fairclough, Tony Rawlings, Karen Amies and Ruth Long at the Cambridge University Map Library.

Bob Hadley for checking the copy and final proof reading.

Finally many thanks to the numerous contributors of photographs both for the main body of the book and for the appendix, and of course to WT (Bill) Stubbs, Alec Swain, Ken Fairey, Sid Nash, Bernard Matthews and Allan Sommerfield for access to their photographic collections.

Once again, many thanks to Shirley for her continued forbearance despite overwhelming mountains of paper and artwork littering the household. Not much longer to go!

Artwork and Design by Paul Smith.

Most shed maps are reproduced from various Ordnance Survey Maps with permission of the Controller of Her Majesty's Stationery Office, © Crown Copyright.

All shed maps are reproduced by permission of The Syndics of Cambridge University Library.

Published by Platform 5 Publishing Ltd., Lydgate House, Lydgate Lane, Sheffield S10 5FH, England.

Printed by Amadeus Press, 517 Leeds Road, Huddersfield, West Yorkshire, HD2 1YJ. Cover by Maxwell Data Management, Slack Lane, Derby.

ISBN 1 872524 05 2

THE
HANDBOOK
OF

BRITISH RAILWAYS

STEAM MOTIVE POWER DEPOTS

PREFACE TO VOLUME 3

It was, perhaps, more than fitting that it was in the north west of England that the steam locomotive finally expired on British Railways and the last steam sheds at Rose Grove, Lostock Hall and Carnforth all closed on Sunday August 4th, 1968 and with it a glorious era came to an end.

It was here, at Rainhill in 1829, that the spark nurtured by Watt, Trevithick, Hedley and then the Stephensons ignited and lit a fire of technological revolution that changed not just Britain but the whole world. Competition to produce a reliable steam locomotive, using little more than iron, leather and wood, for the Liverpool & Manchester Railway gave birth to *The Rocket* and created, not just a new mode of travel, but a driving force for civil & mechanical engineering and metallurgical innovation that became the foundation for todays technology.

This volume looks at the massive concentration of railways that materialised in the north of England, and the motive power depots that served them, in the wake of this expansion of knowledge. The movement of raw materials and finished goods between dock and factory was the key to prosperity for many small railways. Short lines buried into every nook and cranny, linking quarries and mines to the main routes. Many sheds of all shapes and sizes were built over the years to accommodate the huge allocations of locomotives in this area and many survived into BR ownership. This volume also includes, by way of a small bonus, photographs of depots that could not be fitted in in previous volumes and these can be found in Appendix A, towards the back of this book.

The last years of steam had become an embarrassment to a railway network attempting to thrust itself into a new age, the dieselisation programme had proceeded at a ferocious pace, with virtually every manufacturer of locomotives chipping in with one design or another. That the railway needed to change was obvious, management was impatient to be seen to be 'modern'. What caused the greatest distaste was that at the end the steam locomotive died, not gloriously with great ceremony as its proud history demanded, but was swept under the carpet, discarded and bundled out of the back door with scarcely a thank you – A discredited ending to a wonderful chapter of British Engineering.

BRITISH RAILWAYS

PAUL SMITH
Birmingham 1990

BRIDLINGTON MPD (Ken Fairey)

ERRATUM

VOLUME 1

P. 4 For Penicuick read Penicuik
P. 8 For Kinniel read Kinneil
P.20 For 71G read 71G(s)
P.21 The name for No. 34090 should read: Sir Eustace Missenden, Southern Railway.
P.27 Location of 71B(s) Hamworthy Junction should read: In the fork of the Dorchester and Hamworthy lines, west of Hamworthy Junction Station.
P.32 Tiverton Junction Station is now not operational, being replaced by Tiverton Parkway, sited some two miles nearer to Taunton, in 1986.
P.69 Location of 30A(s) Spitalfields should read: At the north end of Spitalfields Coal Depot, south of the line, west of Bethnal Green Station.
Some depots have been misplaced on the County Maps:
P.12 Moorswater should be north west of the mineral line.
P.24 Branksome should be within the triangle.
P.28 Plymouth Dock should be at end of Millbay Line.
P.28 Tiverton Junction should be in the fork of the Exeter and Tiverton Junction lines.
P.54 Margate should be west of the old SER line to Margate Sands.
P.65 Devons Road should be south of the LT&SR main line.
P.65 Ewer Street should be east of the Blackfriars line.
P.65 Stewarts Lane should be south of the Waterloo and Victoria to Clapham Junction lines.
P.82 Barrow Road should be west of the Bristol to South Wales line.
P.82 Dursley should be on the opposite side of the line.
A couple of typographical oddities also occurred:
P.65 A mystery shed appears on the north side of lines near Brixton, and
P.53 The legend 'Bournemouth MPD' appears in a totally incongruous position.

VOLUME 2

P.35 Location of 85A(s) Evesham should read: In the fork of the Oxford and Worcester lines, west of Evesham Station.
P.62 Photograph of Spital Bridge should be credited to *Andrew C. Ingram*
P.86 No. 9022 should be a 4-4-0!
P.108 Holyhead was 7C not 7A
Some depots have been misplaced on the County Maps:
P. 7 Saffron Walden should be east of the line.
P.16 Cromer Beach should be on the north side of the spur
P.24 Felixstowe Beach should be further south, on the opposite side of the line.
P.33 Both Worcester sheds should be inside the triangle
P.38 Shrewsbury should be further north and east of the Severn Valley line and north of the S&M line.
P.38 Clee Hill should be on the opposite side of the line.
P.38 Much Wenlock should be on the opposite side of the line.
P.48 Ross on Wye should be in the fork of the lines.
P.65 Pontypool Road should be south of the cross-valleys line.
P.70 Abercynon should be on the opposite side of the Merthyr line.
P.85 Aberystwyth VR should be west of the Rheidol and Carmarthen lines.
P.105 Llandudno Junction should be west of the Conwy Valley line.
P.105 Croes Newydd should be inside the triangle further north.

BIBLIOGRAPHY

The principal sources of reference for this volume were:
LMS Engine Sheds Vols1 (ISBN 0 906867 02 9), 2 (ISBN 0 906867 05 3), 3 (ISBN 0 906867 07 X) and 4 (ISBN 0 906867 20 7) by Chris Hawkins & George Reeve (Wild Swan Publications)
North Eastern Locomotive Sheds (ISBN 0 7153 5323 3) by K. Hoole (David & Charles)
British Railways Pre-Grouping Atlas and Gazetteer by W.P. Conolly (Railway Publications Ltd)
BR Steam Motive Power Depots NER (ISBN 0 7110 1362 4), ER (ISBN 0 7110 1193 1) and LMR (ISBN 0 7110 1019 6) by Paul Bolger (Ian Allan)
The British Locomotive Shed Directory (1947) by A.L.F. Fuller

BURTON UPON TRENT MPD *(Ken Fairey)*

RETFORD GC MPD *(Ken Fairey)*

THE SHEDS
LISTED BY GEOGRAPHICAL AREA

The country has been divided into 19 Parts and each Part is further sub-divided into Counties and Large Conurbations. These Parts and Sub-Divisions are purely a convenience, based on pre-war County administrations and having no pretensions as to pinpointing towns and villages within "modern" boundaries. BR Regions have been acknowledged, as with regards to the coding of a depot, but each area has been considered as an autonomous unit within which all sheds are dealt with, regardless of origin or operating region. This is designed to present the reader with a complete, concise, rather than fragmented, record of the existence of BR Steam Motive Power Depots within an area.

Each PART is prefaced with a map showing the area covered, indicating all the railway lines built within its boundaries (but not necessarily passing into BR ownership nor, indeed, still extant in 1948) and an index of all the sheds dealt with in that part. Each COUNTY or CONURBATION is prefaced with another map, this time showing the approximate location of each depot relative to the railway network.

Within each sub-division, each FACILITY is identified by name and regional code and LOCATED with reference to nearby stations and lines and pinpointed within about 100 metres by an OS reference. The DIRECTIONS, in the style of Aidan Fullers famous shed directories, are contemporary to its existence. Of all contentious issues with regard to engine sheds, none is more fraught with pot holes than the CLOSURE DATE. Many of those listed are the 'official' ones, but this is by no means decisive. As far as operational requirements went it could have meant an end of a permanent locomotive allocation or permanent staffing, neither of which would have precluded further use of the depot. Indeed, actually closing the building may have just meant that locomotives were serviced and stabled in the yard. Many of the servicing facilities just dwindled away, there being no, nor needing any, "official" date. Hence the OUT OF USE, in many cases no more than just an intelligent stab in the dark.

The DESCRIPTION is of a brief nature, the abbreviation "TS" being shorthand for track straighthouse. The POST CLOSURE HISTORY traces the use of the buildings and site following closure to steam.

Each of the depots is indicated on a reproduction of an ORDNANCE SURVEY MAP, most of these maps are at a scale of 1:5000 and dated as near as possible to 1948. The object is to present a permanent record of the location within a large area, so that although the shed may have long gone the site can be located by reference to other features, roads or buildings. Although the intention of these maps is not to specifically provide accurate track diagrams many do, indeed, provide this information. Where diagrams are of a more recent vintage the depot has been superimposed over its original site, in many instances providing a very interesting contrast. Further commentary, clarifying the location of the site within an area, the adjacency of the local road network, and other points of interest has been added.

Finally, many of the depots have been illustrated by means of a PHOTOGRAPH.

An INDEX, at the end of this volume lists the sheds in alphabetical order and gives a page reference. A complete Index and Bibliography Section for the whole series can be found at the back of *Volume 4.*

A fully coded list of British Railways Motive Power Depots, based upon the first one published in 1950, appears in Volume 1 of this series.

PART TEN
NORTH MIDLANDS

LEICESTERSHIRE NOTTINGHAMSHIRE RUTLAND CHESHIRE LINCOLNSHIRE DERBYSHIRE STAFFORDSHIRE

LEICESTERSHIRE

2A(s) MARKET HARBOROUGH

Location: West of the line, north of Market Harborough Station. (OS Map Ref: SP741876)

Directions: Leave the station by the approach road, turn right under the bridge, right again into Great Bowden Road and a cinder path leads to the shed from a gate on the right hand side.

Closed: October 4th, 1965.

Description: A brick built 2TS through road shed.

Post Closure History: Demolished (1970)

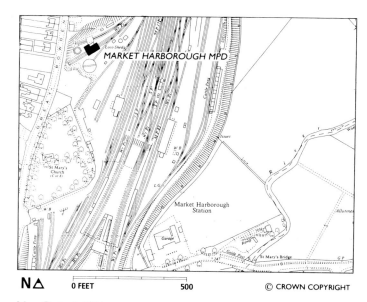

Map Dated: 1961

Site Location: East of the town centre, on the north side of Rockingham Road (A427)

Track Status: Market Harborough Station and line are operational.

The compact design of **MARKET HARBOROUGH MPD**, with the water tank being an integral part of the roof, is clearly evident in this view. A mixture of ex-LMS locomotives occupying the shed building on August 28th, 1960.

WT Stubbs Collection

17C COALVILLE

Location: On the north side of Coalville Town Station. (OS Map Ref: SK426144)
Directions: Turn left outside of the station over the level crossing, cross the line and turn left along a cinder path. This leads to the shed.
Closed: October 4th 1965.
Description: A brick built 3TS shed with 1 through road.
Post Closure History: Demolished. Site of sidings (1981)

A typical scene at **COALVILLE MPD**, dominated by ex-LMS Class 4F 0–6–0 locomotives, on June 14th, 1959.
WT Stubbs Collection

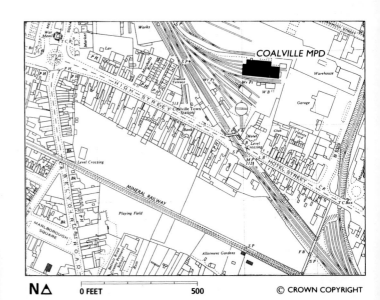

N△   0 FEET   500   © CROWN COPYRIGHT

Map Dated: 1960
Site Location: In the town centre.
Track Status: Coalville station is closed, but the line is operational.

15C LEICESTER MIDLAND

Location: East of the main line, north of Leicester London Road Station. (OS Map Ref: SK597045)
Directions: Turn left outside of the station into London Road, first left into Conduit Street, right at the end into Sparkenhoe Street and left into Upper Conduit Street. Fork left into Upper Kent Street, turn left into Beal Street and the shed entrance is on the left hand side near the end of this road.
Closed: June 13th, 1966 (Steam).
Description: A brick and concrete built circular roundhouse.
Post Closure History: Preserved MR locomotives were housed in the shed immediately after closure, but the main structure was demolished in 1970. The machine shop was converted for diesel use and the depot remains open as a Diesel Depot (Code LR). (1988)

A general view of the yard and shed building at **LEICESTER MIDLAND MPD** on February 26th, 1959. This was one of the few 'modern' depots inherited by BR, having been built on the site of a cluster of semi-derelict shed buildings that lingered

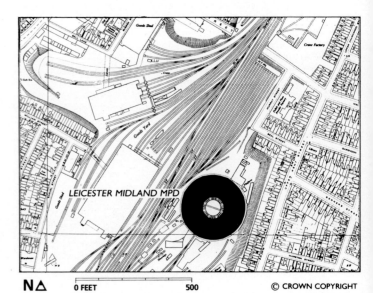

N△   0 FEET   500   © CROWN COPYRIGHT

Map Dated: 1955
Site Location: East of the city centre, on the north side of London Road (A6)
Track Status: Leicester London Road Station and line are operational.

on from MR days. It was during the re-building work, completed by the LMS in 1946, that the former MR roundhouse at Wigston, which closed in 1934, was re-opened to ease the congestion and accommodate and service locomotives from the parent depot at Leicester Midland. After the 'new' depot became fully operational Wigston continued to store and stable engines well into BR days, becoming yet another "unofficial anomaly" *(see Volume 2, Page 28)*, and finally closing in the mid-fifties.
Ken Fairey

38C(s) LEICESTER GN

Location: South of the line, east of Leicester Belgrave Road Station. (OS Map Ref: SK598055)

Directions: Turn left outside of the station, first left into Syston Street and a cobbled path at the end of the road leads through some allotments to the shed.

Closed: June 11th, 1955.

Description: A brick built 3TS dead ended shed, roofless by at least 1953.

Post Closure History: *Demolished. Site occupied by part of Cobden Street. (1990)*

The roofless **LEICESTER GN MPD**, typically housing ex-GN locomotives, nearing the end of its operating days when photographed in 1953.   *WT Stubbs Collection*

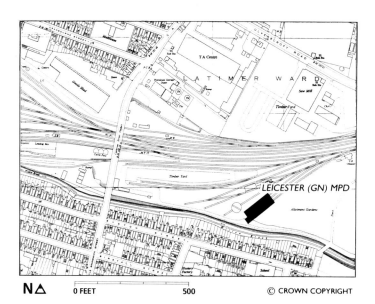

Map Dated: 1955
Site Location: North of the city centre, on the west side of Humberstone Road (A47)
Track Status: Leicester Belgrave Road Station closed in 1957. Line lifted.

38C LEICESTER CENTRAL

Location: East of the line, south of Leicester Central Station. (OS Map Ref: SK579029)

Directions: Turn right outside the station into Great Central Street, right into St. Nicholas Street, proceed along Applegate Street, turn right into West Bridge and continue along Duns Lane, Braunstone Gate and Narborough Road. Turn left into Hopefield Road, continue into Marlow Road, cross the railway bridge and turn left into a cinder path running alongside the track. This path leads to the shed.

Closed: July 6th, 1964.

Description: A brick built 4TS dead ended shed.

Post Closure History: *Demolished. Now site of a timber yard. (1990)*

Class 5MT locomotives in the shape of BR Standard and ex-LNER B1 designs occupy the shed roads at **LEICESTER CENTRAL MPD** on March 12th, 1961. *Ken Fairey*

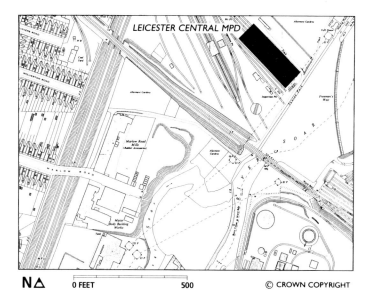

Map Dated: 1955
Site Location: West of the city centre, on the west bank of the River Soar.
Track Status: Leicester Central Station closed in 1969. Line lifted.

17B(s) OVERSEAL

Location: Within the triangle formed by the Moira to Donisthorpe to Gresley lines, at the southern end, west of Moira Station. (OS Map Ref: SK306158)

Directions: From Overseal Village (At the junction of the A444 Nuneaton to Burton Road and the B5004): Take the B5004 towards Swadlincote, for about 1 mile and upon reaching the railway bridge turn right down a Private Road and enter the Goods Yard. Follow the path alongside the yard and a boarded crossing leads to the shed from the left hand side about 400 yards along.

Closed: August 1964.

Description: A brick built 2TS dead ended shed.

Post Closure History: Demolished. Site unused. (1990)

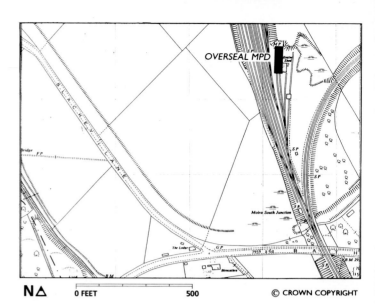

OVERSEAL MPD

OVERSEAL MPD on June 14th, 1959.   *WT Stubbs Collection*

Map Dated: 1961

Site Location: On the north side of Bath Lane (B5003), midway between Overseal and Moira villages.

Track Status: Moira to Gresley line operational. All other lines lifted.

A view of the offices, with turntable alongside, at **NOTTINGHAM VICTORIA MPD**, taken in the early 1960s. Similar facilities existed at many large stations, such as Birmingham New Street, but only this location received an 'official' coding. Yet another component in the 'when is a shed a shed' enigma.   *Chris Bush Collection*

RUTLAND

2A(s) SEATON

Location: In the fork of the Seaton to Luffenham and Peterborough lines, north of Seaton Station. (OS Map Ref: SP912982)
Directions: Entrance to the shed is effected from the station platform.
Out of Use: 1961
Description: A wooden built 1TS dead ended shed.
Post Closure History: Demolished. Now site of scrapyard (1978)

The fire damaged remains of **SEATON MPD**, incredibly still officially in use as a steam shed on August 28th, 1960.   *WT Stubbs Collection*

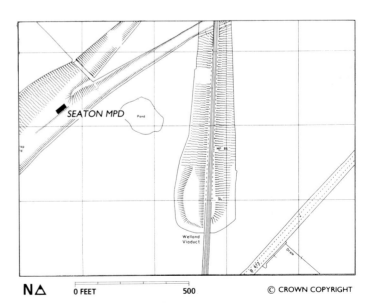

Map Dated: 1976 (Shed Superimposed)
Site Location: East of the village, on the north side of the B672.
Track Status: Seaton Station closed in 1966. Lines lifted.

The shed building was badly damaged by fire on April 27th, 1957

NOTTINGHAMSHIRE

RETFORD (GN) MPD
RETFORD (GC) MPD
TUXFORD JUNCTION MPD
MANSFIELD MPD
KiRKBY BENTINCK MPD
KIRKBY IN ASHFIELD MPD
ANNESLEY MPD
SOUTHWELL MPD
NEWARK MPD
NOTTINGHAM VICTORIA MPD
COLWICK MPD
NOTTINGHAM MPD
TOTON MPD

Scale slightly reduced

16A(s) SOUTHWELL

Location: West of the line, south of Southwell Station. (OS Map Ref: SK708542)
Directions: Entrance to the shed is effected from the station platform.
Closed: January 10th, 1955.
Description: A brick built ITS dead ended shed.
Post Closure History: *Demolished. Site unused (1976)*

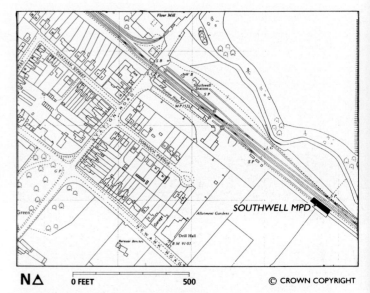

SOUTHWELL MPD

N△   0 FEET   500   © CROWN COPYRIGHT

Map Dated: 1967 (Shed Superimposed)
Site Location: North of the town centre, on the north side of the A612.
Track Status: Southwell Station closed in 1959. Line lifted.

Ex-MR Class 1P 0–4–4T No. 58085, complete with its auto trailer, stands outside of the officially closed **SOUTHWELL MPD** on an August day in 1956.
Allan Sommerfield Collection

16A NOTTINGHAM

Location: South of the line, west of Nottingham Midland Station. (OS Map Ref: SK568389)

Directions: Turn left outside of the station along Carrington Street, right into Queens Bridge Road, right into Waterway Street West and left at the end into Wilford Street. Turn right into Middle Furlong Road and the shed entrance is a gate on the right hand side.

Closed: April 4th, 1965.

Description: A brick built 3 roundhouse shed.

Post Closure History: Demolished. Site now in industrial use. (1990)

A general view of **NOTTINGHAM MPD** in April 1957.

Bernard Matthews Collection

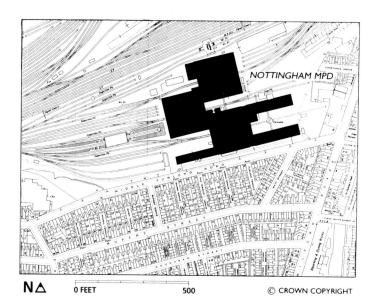

N △   0 FEET   500   © CROWN COPYRIGHT

Map Dated: 1955

Site Location: South of the city centre, on the west side of Wilford Road (B680)

Track Status: Nottingham Midland Station and line are operational.

38B(s) NOTTINGHAM VICTORIA

Location: East of the line, at the south end of Nottingham Victoria Station. (OS Map Ref: SK574402)

Directions: Entrance to the shed is effected from the station platform.

Closed: September 2nd, 1967 (station closure date)

Description: Consisting solely of a turntable and stalls. There are no shed buildings.

Post Closure History: Demolished in September 1967, the whole station site is now occupied by a shopping centre. (1988)

NOTTINGHAM VICTORIA MPD in the early 1960s. The turntable is immediately in front of the buffer on the left hand side, with the offices alongside.

Chris Bush Collection

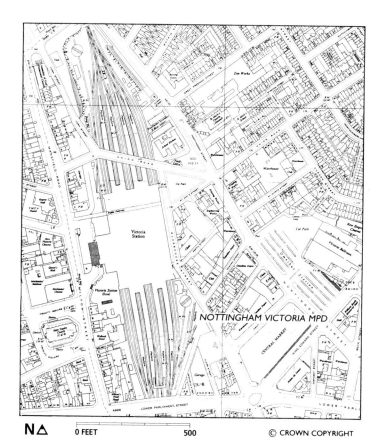

N △   0 FEET   500   © CROWN COPYRIGHT

Map Dated: 1955

Site Location: North of the city centre, adjacent to the north side of Lower Parliament Street (A6008)

A turntable and stalls were also sited at the north end of the station, on the west side of the line.

18A TOTON

Location: West of the line, south of Stapleford & Sandiacre Station. (OS Map Ref: SK486352)

Directions: Turn left out of the station, and almost immediately left again into a small Goods Yard. A cinder path runs alongside the line to the shed from the end of this yard.

Closed: December 1965 (Steam)

Description: A large shed complex consisting of 3 brick built roundhouses.

Post Closure History: *Demolished. The site is now occupied by a purpose built diesel depot (Code TO). (1990)*

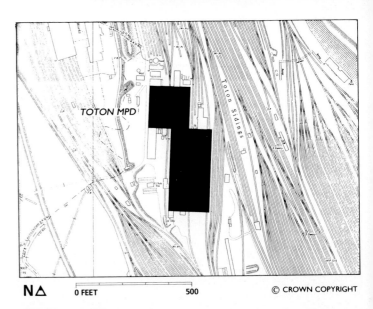

A pre-war view of **TOTON MPD** with some of its allocation of Beyer-Garratts parked in the yard.
Bernard Matthews Collection

Map Dated: 1957

Site Location: South west of Nottingham city centre, on the east side of the A453.

Track Status: Stapleford & Sandiacre Station closed in 1967. Line operational.

16D MANSFIELD

Location: In the triangle of the Mansfield to Sutton Junction to Farnsfield lines, south of Mansfield Station. (OS Map Ref: SK531602)

Directions: Turn sharp left outside of the station into the approach road, turn left into Belvedere Street, proceed along Portland Street and turn right into Quarry Lane. Turn right into Bradder Street and the shed entrance is on the left at the end.

Closed: April 11th, 1960.

Description: A brick built 4TS dead ended shed.

Post Closure History: *Still standing. In use as an engineering workshop, 'Bradder Works' (1990)*

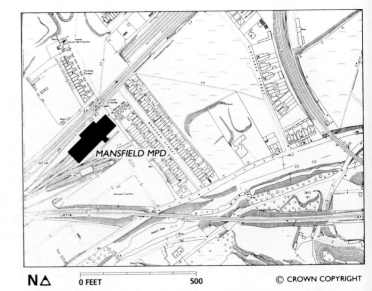

Now finding employment as a Machine Shop, **MANSFIELD MPD** was very much involved in railway business when photographed on July 10th, 1955. *Ken Fairey*

Map Dated: 1958

Site Location: West of the town centre, on the north side of the A615.

Track Status: Mansfield Station closed in 1964. Line operational.

16C KIRKBY IN ASHFIELD

Location: East of the line, north of Kirkby in Ashfield Station. (OS Map Ref: SK505564)

Directions: Turn left along Station Road, at the south of the station, and left into Low Moor Road South. The shed entrance is on the left hand side.

Closed: October 3rd, 1966

Description: Originally a brick built 3TS dead ended shed, enlarged to a 5TS building in 1958.

Post Closure History: *Demolished. Now site of a Skillcentre building and the shed yard is now a Linfood Cash & Carry. (1988)*

An extension to **KIRKBY IN ASHFIELD MPD** was added to the original three road shed, construction commencing in 1958, and this 2TS addition is clearly visible in this view, taken on April 16th, 1961. This portion was utilised for stabling diesel locomotives for a short while after closure to steam.   *WT Stubbs Collection*

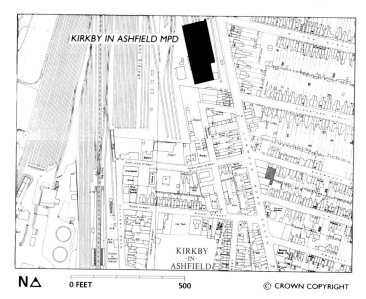

N△   0 FEET   500   © CROWN COPYRIGHT

Map Dated: 1960

Site Location: North of the town centre on the north side of Station Street (B6020)

Track Status: Kirkby in Ashfield Station closed in 1965. Line Operational

38B(s) KIRKBY BENTINCK

Location: In some sidings on the south side of the line, just west of the junction with the Langton Colliery line at the west end of Kirkby Bentinck Station. (OS Map Ref: SK483557)

Directions: Entrance to the shed is effected from the station platform.

Out of Use: 1966

Description: There are no shed buildings. Locomotives stabled on the three lines as and when operating conditions allowed. Principally regarded as a signing-on point.

Post Closure History: *Sidings lifted. Site now landscaped and in agricultural use. The station site is now a horses paddock. (1990)*

A wintry view of **KIRKBY BENTINCK MPD** in BR days. Locomotives stabled beyond the signal box in the distance (visible under the left hand edge of the canopy), water was obtained from the tank and column at the end of the station platform.
Chris Bush Collection

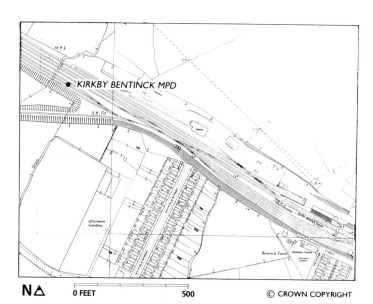

N△   0 FEET   500   © CROWN COPYRIGHT

Map Dated: 1961

Site Location: West of Kirkby in Ashfield, on the west side of Church Hill (B6018)

Track Status: Kirkby Bentinck Station closed in 1963. Lines lifted.

The locomotive with the task of shunting wagons in and out of the nearby Bentinck Colliery (Usually an ex-LNER Class 01 2–8–0) stabled in the sidings between duties during the week, returning to Annesley at the weekend. Water was taken at the station, but any refuelling had to be done at the main depot.

36E RETFORD (GN)

Location: On the west side of Retford Station. (OS Map Ref: SK701802)

Directions: Turn right outside of the station, right again under the subway and enter the second gate on the right, at the top of the steps. Proceed through the Cattle Market, turn right just beyond the Cattle Market Hotel, cross the driveway and the shed entrance is immediately ahead.

Closed: June 14th, 1965.

Description: A brick built 4TS dead ended shed.

Post Closure History: *Still Standing.In use by 'Budge Contractors', the walls of the shed have been rendered smooth and painted white. The building is in excellent condition. (1988)*

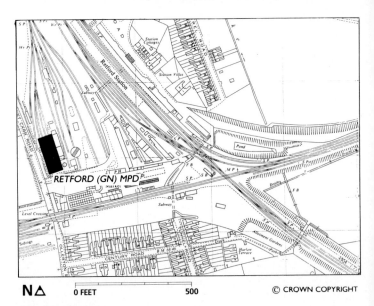

N△   0 FEET   500   © CROWN COPYRIGHT

Map Dated: 1964

Site Location: South of the town centre, on the west side of London Road (A638)

Track Status: Retford Station and lines are operational.

A mixture of diesel and steam locomotives at **RETFORD (GN) MPD** on April 20th, 1965.
Ken Fairey

Both the Retford Sheds were coded 36E!

36E RETFORD (GC)

Location: South of the Retford to Gainsborough line, east of Retford Station. (OS Map Ref: SK708803)

Directions: Turn right outside of the station into a fooootpath running alongside the line. This leads to a level crossing and the shed entrance is on the opposite side of the line.

Closed: January 1965.

Description: A brick built 3TS shed with 2 through roads.

Post Closure History: *Demolished partially to facilitate construction of the east-west diveunder beneath the East Coast Mainline. The remainder of the site is in Industrial use. (1990)*

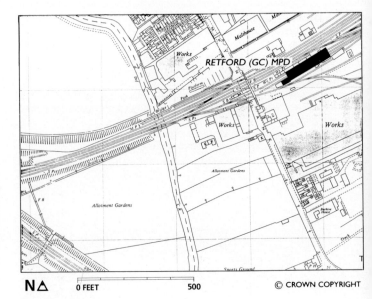

N△   0 FEET   500   © CROWN COPYRIGHT

Map Dated: 1964

Site Location: South of the town centre, on the west side of London Road (A638)

Track Status: Retford Station and lines are operational.

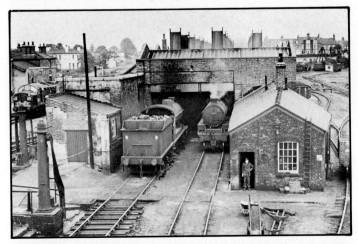

RETFORD (GC) MPD on August 21st, 1964. The Class 37 locomotive, passing on the left of the picture, portends the end of the depot, which duly came less than five months later.
Alec Swain

40D TUXFORD JUNCTION

Location: West of the line, at Dukeries Junction, south of Tuxford Station.
(OS Map Ref: SK749705)
Directions: A road from the eastern side of the Tuxford to Newark road (formerly A1) just north of the ex-GC line overbridge leads to the works and access to the shed is gained by means of a boarded crossing from the works across the GC to GN connecting line.
Closed: February 2nd, 1959.
Description: A brick built 3TS through road shed.
Post Closure History: Demolished. Site unused (1976)

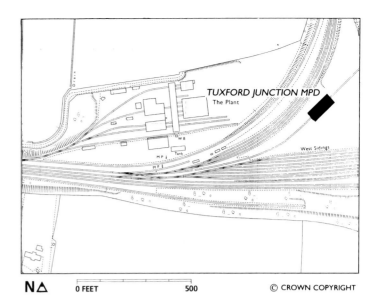

N△   0 FEET   500   © CROWN COPYRIGHT

Map Dated: 1973 (Shed Superimposed)
Site Location: South east of Tuxford village centre.
Track Status: Line operational.

Ex-LNER freight locomotives occupy the shed yard at **TUXFORD JUNCTION MPD** on May 13th, 1956.   *Ken Fairey*

36E(s) NEWARK

Location: On the west side of the line, south of Newark Northgate Station.
(OS Map Ref: SK805540)
Directions: Turn left outside of the station along Lincoln Street, bear right into Appleton Gate and turn left into Sydney Street. Bear left into Lawrence Place and almost immediately turn right along Lawrence Street. Bear left along Newstead Avenue, turn left at the end along Sleaford Road and the shed entrance is on the left hand side a short distance along.
Closed: January 5th, 1959.
Description: A brick built 2TS dead ended shed.
Post Closure History: Demolished. Site in Industrial use. (1988)

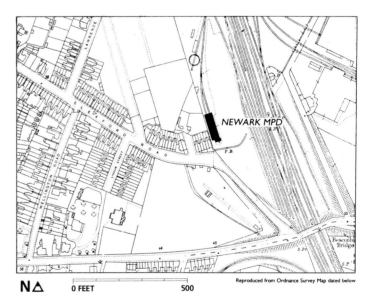

N△   0 FEET   500   Reproduced from Ordnance Survey Map dated below

Map Dated: 1920
Site Location: East of the town centre, on the north side of Sleaford Road (A17)
Track Status: Newark Northgate Station and line are operational.

Ex-MR Class 1P 0–4–4T No. 58085, the Southwell Branch line engine, stands in **NEWARK MPD** shed yard, amongst a small collection of ex-GN types, on April 3rd, 1955.   *Allan Sommerfield Collection*

38A COLWICK

Location: In the fork of the Colwick North Junction to Colwick East and Netherfield & Colwick Station goods lines. (OS Map Ref: SK626409)

Directions: Turn right outside Netherfield & Colwick Station into Meadow Road, turn right at the cross roads into Victoria Road and the shed entrance is on the left hand side just past the level crossing.

Closed: December 12th, 1966.

Description: A brick built 18TS dead ended shed.

Post Closure History: Demolished. Site unused (1981)

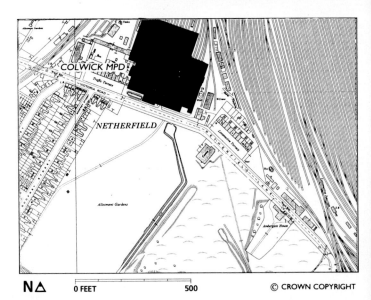

Map Dated: 1954
Site Location: East of Nottingham city centre, south of the A612.
Track Status: Lines lifted.

A distant view of the large shed building at **COLWICK MPD** on September 8th, 1963.
WT Stubbs Collection

38B ANNESLEY

Location: Between the ex-GN Leen Valley and the ex-GC Nottingham to Staveley lines, south of Kirkby in Ashfield. (OS Map Ref: SK525529)

Directions: Leave Newstead (GN) Station by the eastern exit, cross the level crossing and the shed entrance is on the left hand side.

Closed: January 3rd, 1966

Description: A brick built 6TS dead ended shed

Post Closure History: Demolished. The site is now buried under a slag heap. (1990)

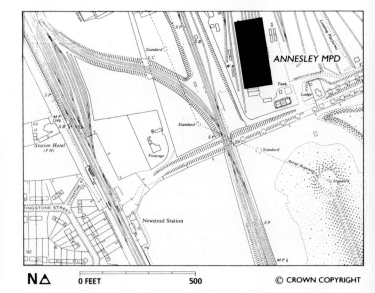

Map Dated: 1961
Site Location: North of Nottingham, on the east side of the A611.
Track Status: Newstead Station closed in 1931. All lines lifted.

Ex-LNER and BR Standard engines monopolise the shed yard at **ANNESLEY MPD** on April 16th, 1961.
WT Stubbs Collection

DERBYSHIRE

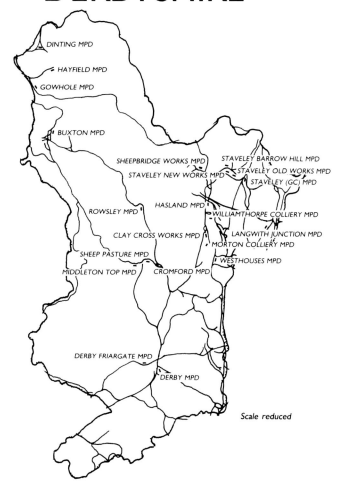

DINTING MPD
HAYFIELD MPD
GOWHOLE MPD
BUXTON MPD
SHEEPBRIDGE WORKS MPD
STAVELEY BARROW HILL MPD
STAVELEY NEW WORKS MPD
STAVELEY OLD WORKS MPD
STAVELEY (GC) MPD
HASLAND MPD
ROWSLEY MPD
WILLIAMTHORPE COLLIERY MPD
CLAY CROSS WORKS MPD
LANGWITH JUNCTION MPD
MORTON COLLIERY MPD
SHEEP PASTURE MPD
WESTHOUSES MPD
MIDDLETON TOP MPD
CROMFORD MPD
DERBY FRIARGATE MPD
DERBY MPD

Scale reduced

18C(s) MORTON COLLIERY

Location: In Morton Colliery on a short spur off the Chesterfield to Nottingham line, about 2 miles south of Clay Cross. (OS Map Ref: SK413603)

Directions: The entrance to the colliery is on the north side of the B6014 in Morton Village and the shed is on the west side of the site.

Closed: June 1948.

Description: A brick built ITS dead ended shed.

Post Closure History: Demolished in December 1966. The shed site is now part of a storage area for motor vehicle bodies. Most of the colliery buildings are still standing. (1990)

A general view of the colliery and shed buildings at **MORTON COLLIERY MPD** taken from an adjacent slag heap during 1957. The depot building can be seen to the right of the chimney. *Reproduced by courtesy of British Coal*

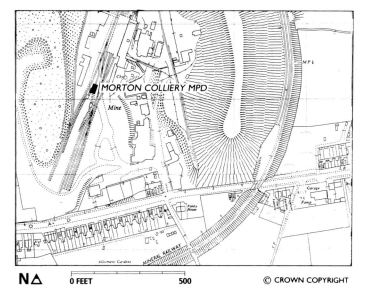

MORTON COLLIERY MPD
Mine
N △   0 FEET   500   © CROWN COPYRIGHT

Map Dated: 1962

Site Location: About 1 mile east of the A61 and 3 miles north of Alfreton.

Track Status: Line operational. All sidings and spur lifted.

The colliery was owned by The Clay Cross Co. Ltd until January 1947 when it was vested in the NCB, East Midlands Division, No. 1 (Bolsover) Area. Locomotives were hired from BR until June 1948 when the NCB acquired a second hand loco to work this site, eliminating the need for a BR engine.

17A DERBY

Location: At the south end of Derby Midland Station, on the east side of the London line. (OS Map Ref: SK364352)

Directions: Cross the station yard into Midland Road and turn left into Carrington Street, left into Nelson Street and right into Noble Street. Turn left into Hulland Street and a footbridge leads to the shed from the end of this street.

Closed: March 1967.

Description: A brick built double-roundhouse

Post Closure History: *Demolished in 1969. A diesel fuelling depot and yard now occupies the site. (1990)*

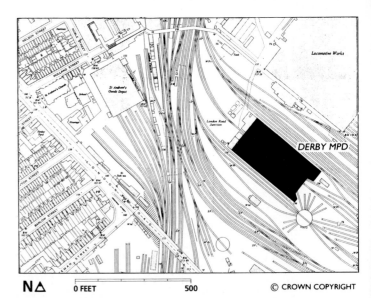

N△   0 FEET   500   © CROWN COPYRIGHT

Map Dated: 1951
Site Location: East of town centre, north of London Road (A6)
Track Status: Derby Station and lines are operational.

A trio of brand new Class 20 Bo–Bo Diesel Electric locomotives outside of **DERBY MPD** on August 16th, 1966. By this time steam had been almost totally supplanted and was limited to a few freight turns.
Ken Fairey

38A(s) DERBY FRIARGATE

Location: North of the line, west of Derby Friargate Station. (OS Map Ref: SK338362)

Directions: Turn left out of the station along Friargate and left again along Uttoxeter Old Road. Turn right into Slack Lane, and the shed entrance is on the left hand side.

Out of Use: 1955

Description: A brick built 4TS dead ended shed

Post Closure History: *Still Standing. In the years immediately following closure it was used for the storing of new DMUs awaiting allocation and was officially regarded as a signing-on point until at least 1959. It is now in industrial use. (1990)*

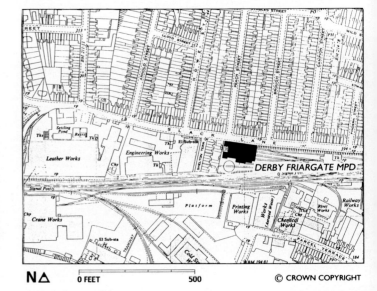

N△   0 FEET   500   © CROWN COPYRIGHT

Map Dated: 1951
Site Location: West of the town centre, north of Uttoxeter New Road (A516)
Track Status: Derby Friargate Station closed in 1964. Line lifted.

Ex-LNER Class J5 0–6–0 No. 65488 and ex-LMS Class 4P 2–6–4T No. 42561 standing outside of a dilapidated roofed **DERBY FRIARGATE MPD** in July 1949.
Allan Sommerfield Collection

9D BUXTON

Location: On the east side of the ex-LNW Stockport line, north of Buxton LNW Station. (OS Map Ref: SK063744)

Directions: Leave the station by the approach road and proceed along the Goods Yard Road. Turn left at the end into Charles Street, left into Lightwood Road and right, just before the railway bridge, into Hogshaw Villas Road. Turn left almost immediately into an opening, enter the gateway at the end and turn right along a cinder path. This path leads to the shed along the top of the embankment.

Closed: March 4th, 1968.

Description: A brick built 6TS dead ended shed.

Post Closure History: *Demolished. Site unused (1990)*

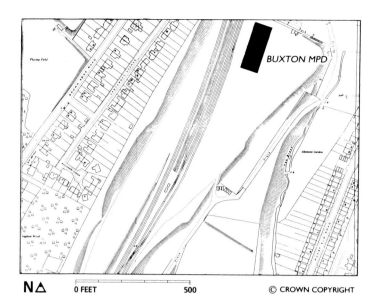

NA   0 FEET   500   © CROWN COPYRIGHT

Map Dated: 1973 (Shed superimposed).
Site Location: North of the town centre, on the west side of the A6.
Track Status: Buxton LNW Station and line are operational.

The large wooden-built shed at **BUXTON MPD** on September 7th, 1960.
WT Stubbs Collection

13C(s) GOWHOLE

Location: On the east side of Gowhole Sidings, on the east side of the Chinley to New Mills line, about 1.5 miles south of New Mills Station. (OS Map Ref: SK015837)

Directions: From Furness Vale Station, adjacent to the east side of the A6: Turn right along Station Road, at the north end of the station, proceed down the hill, bear left at the bottom along Marsh Lane and after a few yards turn sharp right up Ladypit Road, a narrow road leading up a steep hill. Proceed under the two railway bridges and follow the road round to the right. The second of two gates, a short distance on the right hand side, leads into the sidings and the shed is immediately on the left.

Out of Use: March 3rd, 1969. (Closure date of Sidings). It had been regarded as a Signing On Point only from 1959.

Description: Consisting of Engine Pit, 60ft Turntable and Water Column. There are no shed buildings.

Post Closure History: *The whole site is now a nature reserve for blind handicapped children. The turntable pit and engine pit are still clearly visible and it is planned to turn the turntable pit into a duck pond! (1989)*

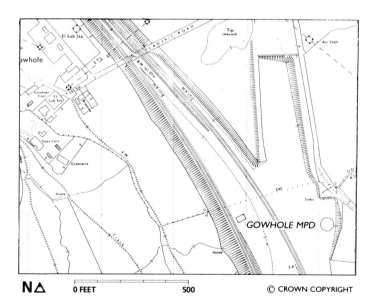

NA   0 FEET   500   © CROWN COPYRIGHT

Map Dated: 1972
Site Location: On the east side of the A6, about 1.5 miles south of New Mills.
Track Status: Sidings Lifted. Line operational.

The turntable and engine pit at the remotely sited **GOWHOLE MPD** on September 7th, 1960.
WT Stubbs Collection

17D ROWSLEY

Location: West of the line, between Darley Dale and Rowsley Stations. (OS Map Ref: SK261640)

Directions: Turn right outside of Rowsley Station and proceed along the A6 Derby Road for about a mile. Turn right into an opening adjacent to Rowsley South Junction Signal Box cross the line by means of the boarded crossing and turn left along a cinder path. This leads to the shed.

Closed: April 27th, 1964.

Description: A brick built 4TS through road shed.

Post Closure History: Demolished. Site unused. (1989)

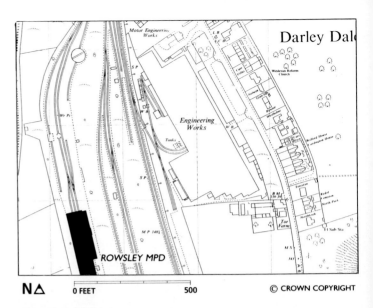

Map Dated: 1967
Site Location: South of Rowsley, on the west side of the A6.
Track Status: Rowsley Station closed in 1967. Line lifted.

ROWSLEY MPD in early BR days.   *Bernard Matthews Collection*

17D(s) CROMFORD

Location: Adjacent to the west side of the canal at the foot of the first incline on the Cromford & High Peak Line. (OS Map Ref: SK313561)

Directions: From the cross roads at Cromford: Follow the A6 towards Derby and after about 1.8 miles cross a railway bridge taking the roadway over the C&HPL. About 50 yards further on turn left through a gateway, this leads to the shed along the side of the line.

Closed: July 26th, 1966. (Steam)

Description: A stone and wooden built 1TS dead ended shed.

Post Closure History: Demolished. The whole line is now the High Peak Nature Trail. (1990)

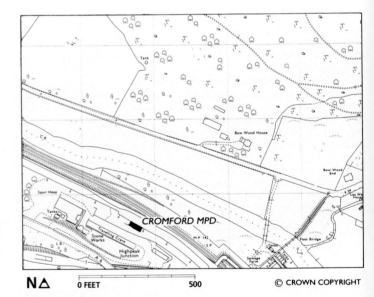

Map Dated: 1970
Site Location: On the north side of the A6, east of Cromford.
Track Status: Lines lifted.

The stone built **CROMFORD MPD**, with wooden extension, on July 10th, 1959. Ex-LNWR tenders were a common sight on the Cromford & High Peak Line, being essential for the transportation of water to various points on the system. *WT Stubbs*

17D(s) MIDDLETON TOP

Location: At the top of the second incline on the Cromford and High Peak Line. (OS Map Ref: SK276552)

Directions: From Wirksworth: Proceed along the Middleton Road (B5023), pass under the bridge carrying the second incline over the road, and turn left at the crossroads at a point called Rise End. Continue under another bridge and bear right along an unmetalled road running up the hillside, turn right along another rough road, and this leads to the shed.

Closed: April 30th, 1967.

Description: A corrugated iron 1TS through road shed.

Post Closure History: Demolished, the site is part of the High Peak Nature Trail. (1990)

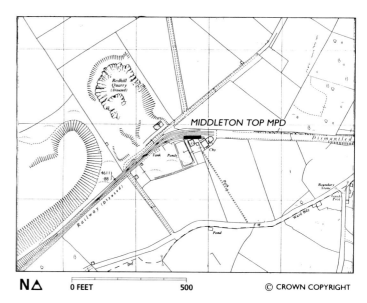

MIDDLETON TOP MPD on July 10th, 1959, housing Class J94 0–6–0ST No. 68006. One of the features of the C&HPR was the variety of odd antiquated tank locomotives that used to find employment, but by this time the 'modern' J94s were in use at Middleton Top and virtually saw out the last days of steam at this location.
WT Stubbs

Map Dated: 1968
Track Status: All lines lifted.

17D(s) SHEEP PASTURE

Location: On the south side of the Cromford and High Peak Line at the top of the first incline. (OS Map Ref: SK300562)

Directions: The most direct route is to climb the first incline from CROMFORD SHED.

Closed: July 26th, 1966. (Steam)

Description: Originally a wooden built 1TS dead ended shed, but during BR days the building was blown down and the depot subsequently consisted of a shed floor and engine pit.

Post Closure History: The floor has been removed and the site forms part of the Cromford and High Peak Nature Trail. (1988)

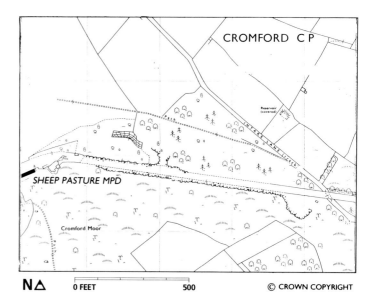

The wooden shed at **SHEEP PASTURE MPD** on July 10th, 1959. After succumbing to a gale, the locomotive (by this time an ex-LMS Kitson 0–4–0ST) parked over the engine pit or in the shed yard between duties. *WT Stubbs Collection*

Map Dated: 1970 (Shed Superimposed)
Site Location: East of Derby Road (A6) and on the south side of the B5036.
Track Status: Line lifted.

39A(s) DINTING

Location: On the south side of Dinting Station. (OS Map Ref: SK022946)
Directions: Entrance to the shed is effected from the station platform.
Closed: 1954 (Steam)
Description: A brick built ITS through road shed
Post Closure History: Still standing. Used as the headquarters of the Dinting Railway Centre, but due to be vacated in September 1990.

DINTING MPD on September 7th, 1960.   *WT Stubbs Collection*

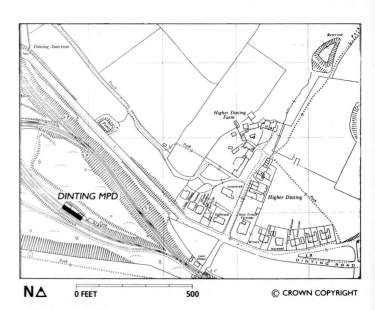

Map Dated: 1968
Site Location: West of Glossop, on the north side of the A6016.
Track Status: Dinting Station and lines are operational.

39A(s) HAYFIELD

Location: On the south side of Hayfield Station. (OS Map Ref: SK036869)
Directions: Entrance to the shed is effected from the station approach road.
Out of Use: 1956
Description: A stone built ITS dead ended shed
Post Closure History: Demolished. The branch line has been converted into a nature trail and the station and shed site is now a car park. The original retaining wall is still intact. (1990)

A DMU waits in the station platform, alongside the abandoned **HAYFIELD MPD**, on November 21st, 1959.   *Alec Swain*

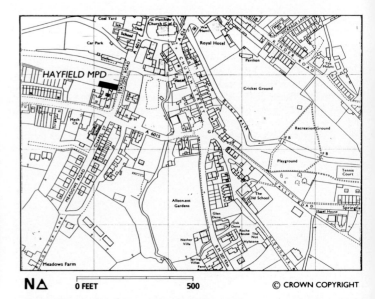

Map Dated: 1972 (Shed Superimposed)
Site Location: In the town centre, on the west side of Station Road (A6015)
Track Status: Hayfield Station closed in 1970. Lines lifted.

18B WESTHOUSES

Location: East of the line, south of Westhouses and Blackwell Station, near the Blackwell Colliery Branch. (OS Map Ref: SK427576)

Directions: Turn left outside the station along the main road and after a short distance turn left again along a rough path. This leads under the lines to the shed.

Closed: October 3rd, 1966 (Steam)

Description: A brick built 6TS dead ended shed.

Post Closure History: *Demolished. Used as a diesel depot (Code WT) until c.1985. Site unused. (1990)*

WESTHOUSES MPD on April 16th, 1961.   *WT Stubbs Collection*

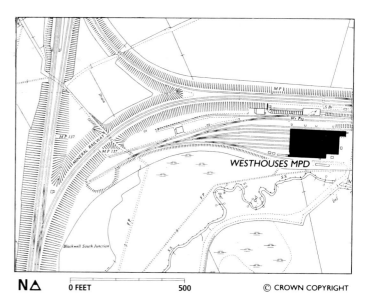

N△   0 FEET   500   © CROWN COPYRIGHT

Map Dated: 1962

Site Location: North of Alfreton, on the south side of Alfreton Road (B6025)

Track Status: Westhouses & Blackwell Station closed in 1967. The Alfreton to Chesterfield line is operational.

40E LANGWITH JUNCTION

Location: West of the Sutton in Ashfield line, south of Shirebrook North Station.(OS Map Ref: SK530684)

Directions: Turn right along the footbridge at the southern end of the station and proceed along East View. Turn left at the end into Langwith Road, left again into Eland Road and the shed entrance is at the end.

Closed: December 1966.

Description: A brick built 2TS shed with one through road, and a brick built 3TS dead ended shed.

Post Closure History: *The 3TS shed has been demolished, whilst the other is still standing in industrial use. (1990)*

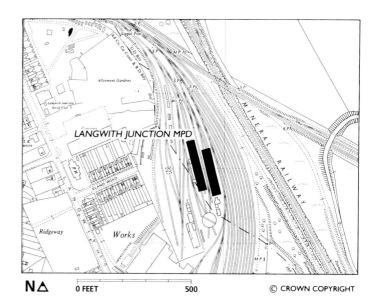

N△   0 FEET   500   © CROWN COPYRIGHT

Map Dated: 1959

Site Location: On the east side of Langwith Road, south of the A632.

Track Status: Shirebrook North Station closed in 1955. Line lifted.

LANGWITH JUNCTION MPD on April 16th, 1961.   *WT Stubbs Collection*

18D STAVELEY BARROW HILL

Location: On the south side of a freight line at Barrow Hill. (OS Map Ref: SK412754)

Directions: Turn left outside of Barrow Hill Station along Station Road, turn right at the crossroads and immediately enter a gateway on the left hand side. This is a private road which leads to the shed.

Closed: October 4th, 1965 (Steam)

Description: A brick built roundhouse.

Post Closure History: *Still Standing. Used as a Diesel Depot (Code BH) until 1987. Now in use as a Stabling Point, but closure threatened. (1990)*

STAVELEY BARROW HILL·MPD on October 22nd, 1963. After closure to steam the depot found fame as the last roundhouse still in use for locomotive purposes on BR. It was due to close completely in October 1990 after 120 years of service.
WT Stubbs Collection

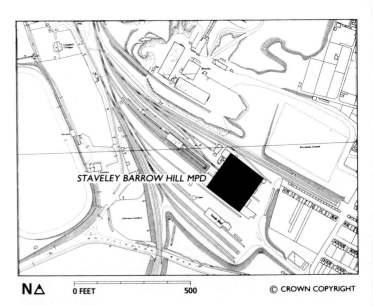

N△   0 FEET   500   © CROWN COPYRIGHT

Map Dated: 1962

Site Location: North west of the town centre, on the north side of Whittington Road.

Track Status: Barrow Hill Station closed in 1954. Line operational.

38D STAVELEY (GC)

Location: East of the line, south of Staveley Central Station. (OS Map Ref: SK436744).

Directions: Leave the station, cross over the road and proceed along Railway Cottages. Turn right into an opening, just as the roadway bears left, climb the railway embankment by the railway bridge and this leads to the shed.

Closed: June 14th, 1965

Description: Formerly a brick built 12TS dead ended shed, rebuilt to a 5TS structure in 1952.

Post Closure History: *Demolished. Unused.*

A typically smoky scene at **STAVELEY (GC) MPD** on October 22nd, 1963.
WT Stubbs Collection

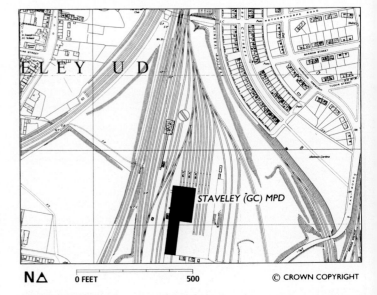

N△   0 FEET   500   © CROWN COPYRIGHT

Map Dated: 1962

Site Location: East of the town centre, on the south side of Lowgates (A619)

Track Status: Staveley Central Station closed in 1963. Line operational.

18D(s) STAVELEY NEW WORKS

Location: In Staveley New Works. (OS Map Ref: SK413748)
Directions: Leave Staveley Works Station by the northern exit and turn left along Works Road. Turn left into the Main Gate, and the shed is within the works complex.
Closed: October 4th, 1965.
Description: A brick built 2TS dead ended shed.
Post Closure History: *Still Standing. In use for the storage and maintenance of contractors vehicles.(1990).*

Ex-MR Class 0F 0–4–0T No. 41529 stands outside of **STAVELEY NEW WORKS MPD**, alongside one of Stanton & Staveley's own locomotives and amid a mountain of pipe couplings, at sometime in the late 1950s. The shed still stands, little altered from the condition shown in the photograph.   *Chris Bush Collection*

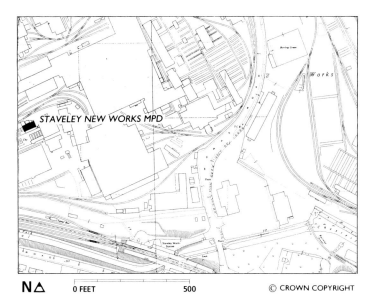

N△   0 FEET   500   © CROWN COPYRIGHT

Map Dated: 1962
Site Location: North west of town centre. Staveley New Works occupies the site on the west side of Works Road.
Track Status: Staveley Works Station closed in 1963. Line lifted. All lines lifted in works area.

18D(s) STAVELEY OLD WORKS

Location: In Staveley Devonshire Works. (OS Map Ref: SK419751)
Directions: Leave Staveley Works Station by the northern exit and turn left along Works Road. Turn right into Gate 5, cross the river and follow the works road for a short distance. The shed is on the left hand side.
Closed: October 4th, 1965.
Description: A brick built 2TS through road shed.
Post Closure History: *Demolished. Site now occupied by a lorry park. (1990)*

Ex-MR Class 1F 0–6–0T No. 41763 shunts wagons in Devonshire Works on April 20th, 1965. The slightly mis-nomered brick built **STAVELEY OLD WORKS MPD** can be observed at the rear of the car park, alongside the gasholder.
          Ken Fairey

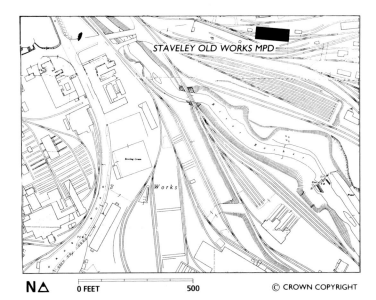

N△   0 FEET   500   © CROWN COPYRIGHT

Map Dated: 1962
Site Location: North west of town centre. Staveley Old Works is located on the east side of the road and south of the River Rother. The Devonshire Works occupies the remainder of the easternmost site, north of the river.
Track Status: Staveley Works Station closed in 1963. Line lifted. All lines lifted in works area.

The Staveley New and Old Works sites are now owned by Stanton PLC. Staveley Devonshire Works are now owned by Staveley Chemicals

18C HASLAND

Location: On the east side of the Clay Cross line, about 1.75 miles south of Chesterfield Station. (OS Map Ref: SK 391685)

Directions: Bear left outside the station into Corporation Street, turn left into St. Mary's Gate, continue into Lordsmill Street and fork right into Derby Road (A61). After about 1 mile, turn left into Storforth Lane and turn right into North Terrace, just past the bridge. Turn left at the end and a road almost immediately on the right hand side leads to the shed.

Closed: September 7th, 1964.

Description: A brick built roundhouse. Local subsidence had necessitated removal of part of the roof and was in a very dilapidated condition by closure.

Post Closure History: *Demolished. Site unused.*

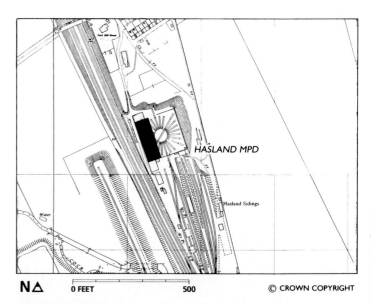

HASLAND MPD suffered very badly from subsidence necessitating removal of the roof some time before closure. This view of an ex-LMS Class 5 4–6–0 parked in front of the shell of the building was taken on October 22nd, 1963.
WT Stubbs Collection

Map Dated: 1962
Site Location: South of Chesterfield, on the east side of the A61.
Track Status: Chesterfield Station and line are operational.

18C(s) CLAY CROSS WORKS

Location: In the fork of the Chesterfield to Derby and Alfreton lines at Clay Cross Works. (OS Map Ref: SK4006444)

Directions: The A6175 runs in a north easterly direction from its junction with the A61 at Clay Cross. The entrance to the works is on the left hand side, about 1 mile along, just before a railway bridge.

Closed: 1954 *(End of hiring arrangement from BR)*

Description: A brick built 1TS through road shed.

Post Closure History: *The original shed was demolished and rebuilt for stabling two works owned diesel shunting locomotives. Building now in use, housing compressors. (1990)*

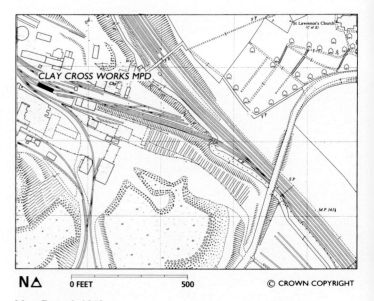

The unbelievably decrepit shed at **CLAY CROSS WORKS MPD** containing ex-MR Class 1F 0–6–0T No. 41763 in August 1954, the last year of BR operation. The building actually lasted until the early 1970s when it was demolished and replaced by a new 1TS structure. This itself became redundant when the internal rail system ceased operation on March 1st, 1978 and is now in use as a Compressor House.
Photomatic

Map Dated: 1962
Track Status: All lines lifted.
The site is now owned by Biwater Pipes & Castings Ltd. Large parts of the original works buildings are still in situ.

18C(s) WILLIAMTHORPE COLLIERY

Location: The Stabling Point is south of the line at the west end of the colliery yard.(OS Map Ref: SK424664)

Directions: From Holmewood: Follow Chesterfield Road (B6039) in a northwards direction from its junction with the A6175 and after about a half mile, just before a railway bridge, turn right along a private road. Turn left into the colliery and follow the railway lines to the left. The stabling point is at the end of these short sidings.

Closed: October 6th, 1967. *(End of leasing arrangement)*

Description: Consisting of a Water Tank and Engine Pit. There are no shed buildings.

Post Closure History: *The colliery buildings, although closed in 1970, remain intact. The shed site is now part of a field. (1990)*

Ex-LMS 'Jinty' 0–6–0T locomotives Nos 47629 and 47289 take a breather between duties at **WILLIAMTHORPE COLLIERY MPD** on May 20th, 1967.
Ken Fairey

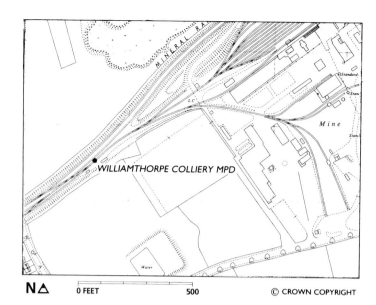

Map Dated: 1962
Site Location: North of Holmewood, on the east side of the B6039.
Track Status: All lines lifted.
Engines were allocated in pairs, working 24 hours/day on a 25 day rota. They shunted individually in the colliery yard and every couple of hours double-headed a load from the washing plant towards the main line.

18D(s) SHEEPBRIDGE WORKS

Location: Within the Sheepbridge Works on the north side of the line. (OS Map Ref: SK374748)

Directions: Broombank Road leads in a westerly direction off Sheffield Road (A61) about 1 mile north of Chesterfield. Follow this road and turn left along Sheepbridge Lane. Cross the small river bridge and the works entrance is on the left, a short distance before a level crossing. Proceed past the right hand side of the main works building and the shed is adjacent to the line.

Closed: 1965

Description: Originally a brick built 2TS dead ended shed, demolished by 1948. The locomotives stabled on the former shed roads, with a simple lean-to shelter provided over the southernmost track, the engine pit still in situ on the northern track.

Post Closure History: *Used for private diesel shunters after closure to BR. Lines lifted in November 1975. Site now in use as an Industrial Estate with a few of the original works buildings still standing. (1990)*

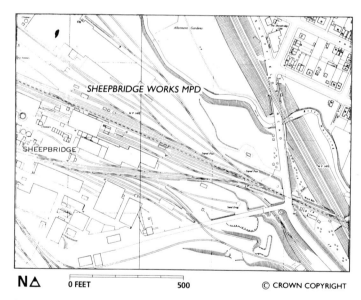

Map Dated: 1965
Track Status: All lines lifted.

The simple corrugated iron cantilevered structure at **SHEEPBRIDGE WORKS MPD** some time after closure in the mid-sixties.
RO Gratton

CHESHIRE

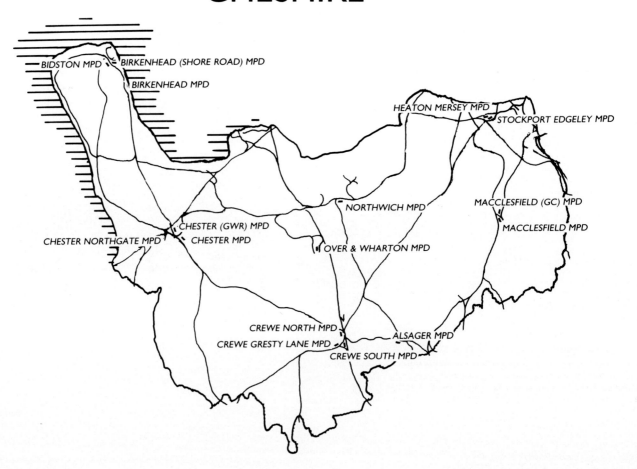

6A CHESTER

Location: On the north side of the Chester to Crewe line, east of Chester Station. (OS Map Ref: SJ423667)

Directions: Turn right outside of Chester General Station and ascend the flight of steps to Hoole Road, turning right over the end of the station and turn right again into Lightfoot Street. Turn right at the end into Station View, crossing the railway, turn sharp left into Hoole Lane, re-crossing the railway and a cinder path leads to the shed from the right hand side, just past the bridge.

Closed: June 5th, 1967.

Description: A brick built 8TS dead ended shed.

Post Closure History: *Demolished. Now site of a housing estate. (1990)*

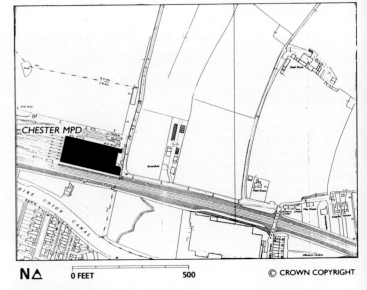

CHESTER MPD

N△   0 FEET   500   © CROWN COPYRIGHT

Map Dated: 1961

Site Location: East of the town centre, on the north side of the A51.

Track Status: Chester Station and lines are operational.

An ex-GWR 0–6–0PT locomotive is surrounded by ex-LMS varieties in a very full **CHESTER MPD** shed yard on April 24th, 1960.

Alec Swain

84K CHESTER (GWR)

Location: On the east side of the Chester to Birkenhead line, north of Chester General Station.(OS Map Ref: SJ410672)

Directions: Turn right outside the station, climb the steps to Hoole Road, turning right over the end of the station, and enter the Goods Yard approach road on the left hand side. A footbridge leads from the left hand side of this road to the shed.

Closed: April 10th, 1960 (steam).

Description: A complex consisting of a brick built 3TS through road shed and a brick built 3TS through road shed of LNWR origin. The latter shed was rebuilt by BR during the mid-fifties.

Post Closure History: *Still Standing. In use as a diesel depot (Code CH).*

A contrast in depot buildings at **CHESTER (GWR) MPD** on May 1st, 1960, with a vintage 0–6–0 Diesel Shunter standing outside of the ageing ex-GWR shed *(above)*, whilst the builders reconstruct the floor of the ex-LNWR portion, some three years after the re-roofing had been completed if the graphically inept '1957' is to be believed *(below)* WT Stubbs

6D CHESTER NORTHGATE

Location: In the Goods Yard on the east side of Chester Northgate Station. (OS Map Ref: SJ406671)

Directions: A flight of steps leads from the east side of Northgate Station yard into the Goods Yard, and a cobbled path leads around the perimeter of the yard to the shed.

Closed: January 4th, 1960 (Steam).

Description: A brick built 2TS dead ended shed

Post Closure History: *Demolished. Site redeveloped (1990)*

CHESTER NORTHGATE MPD was utilised as a DMU Depot after closure as this view, taken on May 1st, 1960, shows. *WT Stubbs*

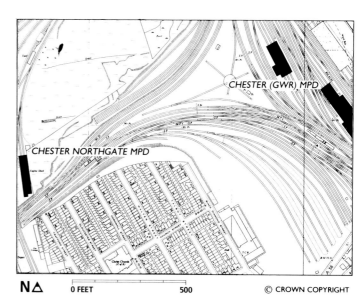

Map Dated: 1959

Site Location: North of the town centre, on the north side of Brook Street (A56)

Track Status: Chester Station and lines are operational.
Chester Northgate Station closed in 1969. Line lifted.

5A CREWE NORTH

Location: On the west side of the line at the north end of Crewe Station. (OS Map Ref: SJ709550)

Directions: A footbridge leads from the north end of Platform 1 to the shed.

Closed: May 25th 1965

Description: A complex consisting of brick built 4TS and 12TS dead ended adjoining sheds, with a post war built 8 track semi-roundhouse shed.

Post Closure History: *Demolished. Site now in use as a car park. (1990)*

A general view of the large depot at **CREWE NORTH MPD** on May 29th, 1960.
WT Stubbs Collection

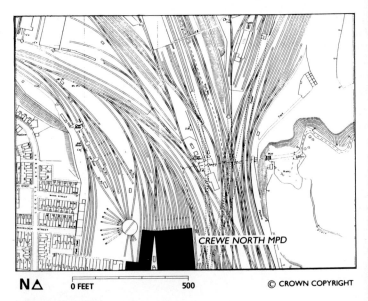

CREWE NORTH MPD

N△   0 FEET   500   © CROWN COPYRIGHT

Map Dated: 1961
Site Location: South of town centre, on the north side of the A5020.
Track Status: Crewe Station and lines are operational

5B CREWE SOUTH

Location: In the fork of the Stafford and Shrewsbury lines, south of Crewe Station. (OS Map Ref: SJ714538)

Directions: Turn left outside of Crewe Station main entrance, and almost immediately turn left through a gate into the goods yard. Follow the drive through the yard and at the end cross the railway by means of the boarded level crossing. A cinder path leads to the shed from this crossing.

Closed: November 6th, 1967.

Description: Originally a brick built 12TS through road shed, but latterly reduced to 8 roads.

Post Closure History: *Demolished. Now sidings as part of South Yard. (1990)*

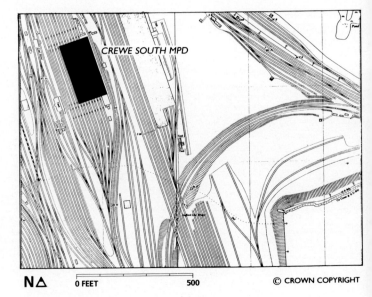

CREWE SOUTH MPD

N△   0 FEET   500   © CROWN COPYRIGHT

Map Dated: 1961
Site Location: South of town centre, on the south side of the A5020.
Track Status: Crewe Station and lines are operational

Whilst Crewe North MPD handled all the top link passenger turns **CREWE SOUTH MPD** was principally assigned to freight duties. The depot and shed yard, viewed on September 9th, 1962, shows a typical collection of ex-LMS mixed traffic and freight locomotives.
Ken Fairey

84H(s) CREWE GRESTY LANE

Location: On the north side of the Shrewsbury line, west of Crewe Station. (OS Map Ref: SJ707536)

Directions: Leave the station by the main entrance and turn left. Turn left into Gresty Lane and proceed along until a railway overbridge is reached. A cinder path on the right hand side, just before the bridge leads to the shed.

Closed: June 17th, 1963.

Description: A brick built 2TS dead ended shed.

Post Closure History: Demolished. Now site of industrial estate. (1990)

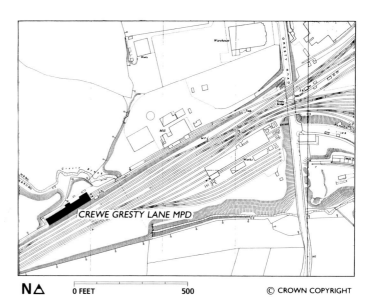

Map Dated: 1961
Site Location: South of town centre, on the south side of the A5020.
Track Status: Crewe Station and lines are operational.

The GW interloper, **CREWE GRESTY LANE MPD** on May 29th, 1960. Despite the presence of the massive ex-LMS depots it, amazingly, never fell victim to 'rationalisation' and closed only a few months before Crewe North.
WT Stubbs Collection

5A(s) OVER & WHARTON

Location: West of the line, north of Over & Wharton Station. (OS Map Ref: SJ656665)

Directions: Entrance to the shed is effected from the station platform

Closed: August 30th, 1947, and subsequently used as a Stabling Point until c1964.

Description: A brick built 1TS dead ended shed.

Post Closure History: Demolished, Site unused (1972)

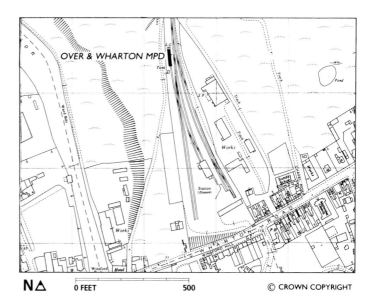

Map Dated: 1964 (Shed Superimposed)
Site Location: On the east bank of the River Weaver, adjacent to the north side of Wharton Road (A5018)
Track Status: Over & Wharton Station closed in 1947. Line lifted.

Ex-LNER Class C13 4–4–2T No. 67436 stands alongside the water tower, in front of the remnants of **OVER & WHARTON MPD** on October 17th, 1953.
WT Stubbs Collection

9C MACCLESFIELD

Location: East of the Prestbury line, about 500 yards north of Macclesfield Station. (OS Map Ref: SJ918741)

Directions: Turn right outside of the station, go under the railway bridge and proceed along Gas Road. A gateway, opposite the end of this road leads to the shed through the Goods Yard.

Closed: June 12th, 1961.

Description: A brick built 3TS through road shed, latterly roofless.

Post Closure History: Demolished, the floors are still traceable, and the whole site is now a coal yard. (1988)

Ex-LMS Tank Engines, the staple diet of the former NSR depot, occupy the building at **MACCLESFIELD MPD** on October 25th, 1959.   *WT Stubbs Collection*

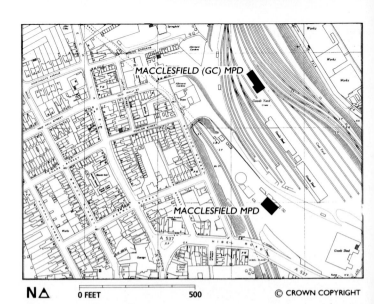

N△   0 FEET   500   © CROWN COPYRIGHT

Map Dated: 1965 (Both Sheds Superimposed)

Site Location: North of the town centre, on the north side of Hibel Road (A537)

Track Status: Macclesfield Station and Stoke to Manchester line operational. All other lines lifted.

39A(s) MACCLESFIELD (GC)

Location: On the west side of the ex-GC Macclesfield to Maple line, north of Macclesfield Station. (OS Map Ref: SJ918742)

Directions: As for MACCLESFIELD shed. the depot is at the far end of the Goods Yard.

Closed: 1933, and subsequently used as a stabling point until c.1950.

Description: A brick built 2TS through road shed.

Post Closure History: Demolished. Site unused (1988).

The substantial two road brick built shed at **MACCLESFIELD (GC) MPD** in pre-BR days. Used as a Stabling Point until nationalisation, when at some point, so far undetermined, all locomotive matters passed over to the nearby ex-NSR establishment and the shed fell into disuse.   *WT Stubbs Collection*

Classes 08, 24 and 40 locomotives share the accomodation with BR Class 4MT 2–6–4T No. 80079 and ex-SR Merchant Navy Class 4–6–2 No. 35028 *CLAN LINE*, as the depot at **NORTHWICH MPD** once again plays host to steam locomotives on May 18th, 1980.

Many former steam sheds found themselves pressed into service as diesel depots in the early years of total dieselisation, most of them for just a few months or years as the more specialised structures, with split level maintenance bays and superior working conditions, were opened. The steam sheds were basically unchanged yet, surprisingly, a few still enjoy an extended existence in their 'new' role. Depots such as Northwich, above, Birkenhead and Westhouses have only recently fallen by the wayside, whilst Doncaster, Grangemouth and Motherwell, amongst others still survive, outlasting by many years purpose built Diesel Depots such as Finsbury Park. Many of these depots, built in the wake of the dieselisation programme, fell victim to the drastic changes in passenger train haulage and freight traffic operation. It is no coincidence that the majority of the remaining former steam sheds are used for the servicing of the principal freight classes of locomotives.   *Sid Nash*

9B STOCKPORT EDGELEY

Location: West of the line, south of Stockport Edgeley Station. (OS Map Ref: SJ892892)

Directions: Go straight ahead outside of the station along Station Road, turn right into Wellington Road, right into Greek Street, left into Shaw Heath, right into Booth Street and a gate on the left hand side leads to the shed along a cinder path.

Closed: May 6th, 1968.

Description: A brick built 8TS dead ended shed.

Post Closure History: Demolished. Site unused. (1980)

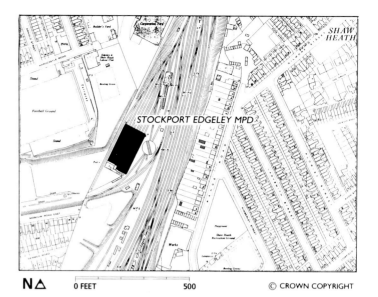

Ex-LMS Class 5 4–6–0s are well represented in this view of **STOCKPORT EDGELEY MPD**, taken on May 21st, 1966. *Bernard Matthews Collection*

Map Dated: 1960

Site Location: South of the town centre, on the west side of Bramhall Lane (A5102)

Track Status: Stockport Edgeley Station and line are operational.

13C HEATON MERSEY

Location: At the south side of the fork of the Cheadle and Didsbury lines, west of Tiviot Dale Station. (OS Map Ref: SJ878900)

Directions: From Stockport Edgeley Station: Go ahead outside of the station along Station Road, turn left into Wellington Road, descend the flight of steps into Mersey Square and proceed westwards along Chestergate. Continue into Brinksway and Stockport Road and after about 1 mile turn right into Gorsey Bank Road. A cinder path leads from the right hand side across a river and to the shed.

Closed: May 6th, 1968.

Description: A brick built 8TS dead ended shed.

Post Closure History: Demolished. Site occupied by industrial units. (1990)

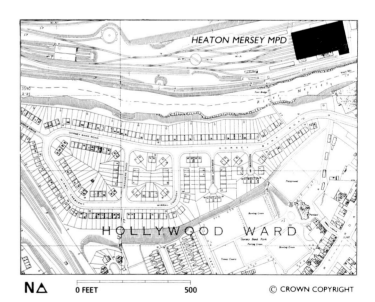

A busy scene at **HEATON MERSEY MPD** on September 27th, 1959.
WT Stubbs Collection

Map Dated: 1960

Site Location: West of Stockport town centre, on the north bank of River Mersey.

Track Status: The Cheadle line is operational.

5E ALSAGER

Location: On the south side of the line, east of Alsager Station. (OS Map Ref: SJ806552)
Directions: Turn left outside the station along Talke Road and a cinder path leads to the shed from the left hand side a short distance along.
Closed: June 18th, 1962.
Description: A brick built 4TS dead ended shed.
Post Closure History: Demolished. (1990)

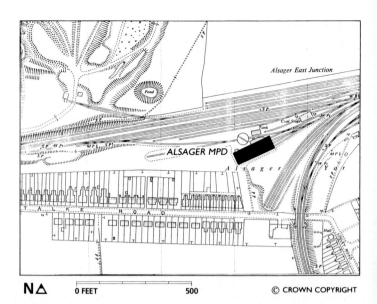

N△   0 FEET   500   © CROWN COPYRIGHT

Map Dated: 1954
Site Location: South of the town centre, on the south side of the B5077.
Track Status: Alsager Station and line are operational.

Ex-LMS Class 4F 0–6–0 locomotives Nos 44386 and 44595 stand in the entrance to **ALSAGER MPD** on February 14th, 1960.   *Ken Fairey*

13D NORTHWICH

Location: On the south side of Northwich Station. (OS Map Ref: SJ670739)
Directions: Go straight ahead outside of the station along the approach road, turn sharp left into Middlewich Road, cross the bridge and the shed entrance is on the left hand side.
Closed: March 4th, 1968 (Steam)
Description: A brick built 4TS dead ended shed.
Post Closure History: Still Standing. Used as a diesel depot (Code NW) until 1987, but since abandoned. (1990)

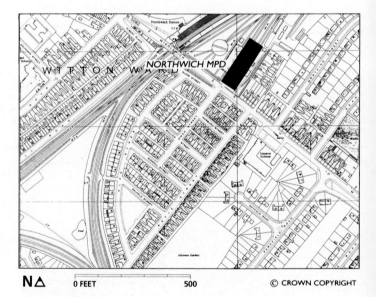

N△   0 FEET   500   © CROWN COPYRIGHT

Map Dated: 1965
Site Location: East of the town centre, on the north side of Middlewich Road (B5082)
Track Status: Northwich Station and line are operational.

NORTHWICH MPD on September 24th, 1961. Few alterations were made when it became a Diesel Depot in 1968 and looked much the same throughout its extended career.   *Ken Fairey*

6C BIRKENHEAD

Location: At the end of a spur on the west side of the Chester line, about 1200 yards south of Birkenhead Woodside Station. (OS Map Ref: SJ323882)

Directions: Turn left outside of Birkenhead Woodside Station along Chester Street and turn right into Grange Road and the turn left into Argyle Street. Proceed into Argyle Street South, passing Birkenhead Central Station, turn left into Mollington Street and the shed entrance is a door at the end.

Closed: November 6th, 1967 (Steam). November 24th, 1985 (Totally)

Description: A brick built 16TS dead ended shed.

Post Closure History: Used as a diesel depot (Code BC) until 1985 and demolished in July 1987. Site unused. (1990)

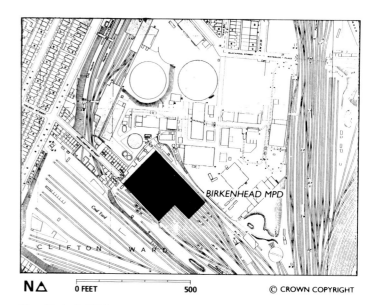

Map Dated: 1955

Site Location: South of town centre, on the west side of the A41.

Track Status: Birkenhead Station and line are operational.

BIRKENHEAD MPD was a joint shed of GWR and LMS origin and this is illustrated by the presence of locomotives from both former companies on March 21st, 1954, the ex-GWR 5101 Class 2–6–2T No. 4129 still retaining its pre-BR livery.

Ken Fairey

13E(s) BIRKENHEAD (SHORE ROAD)

Location: South of the line, west of Shore Road Goods Station. (OS Map Ref: SJ323895))

Directions: Leave Birkenhead Woodside Station, cross over Chester Street and proceed along Shore Road. Follow the road around to the left and the shed entrance is on the left hand side, just past the level crossing, at its junction with Canning Street.

Closed: June 5th, 1961

Description: A wooden built 1TS dead ended shed.

Post Closure History: Upon BR closure continued in use for stabling private shunters.

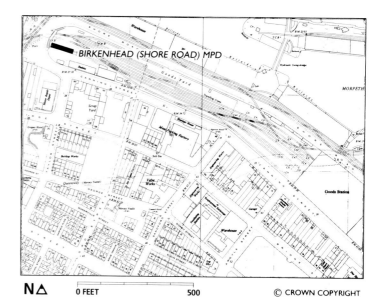

Map Dated: 1955

Site Location: North of the town centre, on the south side of Morpeth Dock.

Track Status: Most lines lifted

The obscure **BIRKENHEAD SHORE ROAD MPD** on October 22nd, 1961. By this time the dilapidated shed had ceased to be a BR depot and was solely in use for private shunters. *WT Stubbs Collection*

6F BIDSTON

Location: On the west side of the line, north of Birkenhead North Station. (OS Map Ref: SJ294904)

Directions: Turn right outide Birkenhead North Station into Station Road and right again into Wallasey Bridge Road. A path leads to the shed from the left hand side, just before the overbridge.

Closed: February 11th, 1963.

Description: A brick built 2TS dead ended shed.

Post Closure History: Demolished.

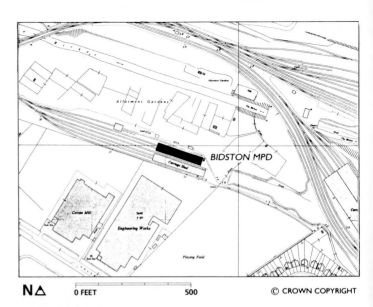

Map Dated: 1954
Site Location: West of Birkenhead town centre.
Track Status: Bidston Station and lines are operational.

BIDSTON MPD on July 2nd, 1961.   *WT Stubbs Collection*

Ex-LMS Class 5 4–6–0 No. 45318 is the centre of attraction as it stands on the turntable at **LOSTOCK HALL MPD** on August 3rd, 1968. Later in the day it took charge of the last timetabled steam hauled train, the 21.25 Preston to Liverpool, as anonymous and derisive a working as could be found for such an historic occasion, and with it BR were finally able to wash their hands of their perceived grimy outmoded image.
CA Hibbert

STAFFORDSHIRE

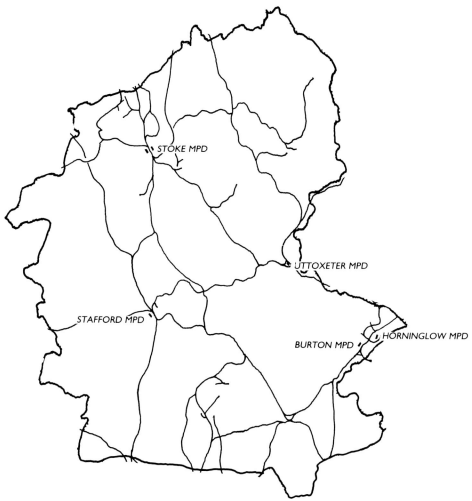

5C STAFFORD

Location: West of the line, at the north end of Stafford Station. (OS Map Ref: SJ916231)

Directions: Turn left outside of the station along Railway Street, left along Castle Street, cross the railway bridge and the shed entrance is on the left hand side.

Closed: July 19th, 1965.

Description: A brick built 6TS dead ended shed.

Post Closure History: Still Standing. The roof has been replaced and it is now in commercial use as 'The Palmbourne Industrial Park' (1990)

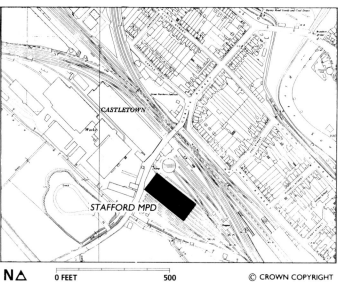

N△   0 FEET   500   © CROWN COPYRIGHT

Map Dated: 1960

Site Location: West of the town centre, on the north side of Victoria Road (B5025)

Track Status: Stafford Station and line are operational.

STAFFORD MPD on April 22nd, 1962.   *WT Stubbs*

5D STOKE

Location: On both sides of the line at the junction of the Stoke to Stone and Uttoxeter lines, south of Stoke Station. (OS Map Ref: SJ883449)

Directions: Turn right outside of the station along Winton Square, right under the railway bridge along Glebe Street, left along Wharf Street, left into City Road and after about 50 yards turn right into a short road. This leads to the shed.

Closed: August 7th, 1967.

Description: Consisting of a brick built 8TS shed, with 7 through roads, on the east side of the line, and a brick built roundhouse on the west.

Post Closure History: *Demolished. The roundhouse is now the site of a DIY warehouse and the straight sheds site of commercial development. (1990)*

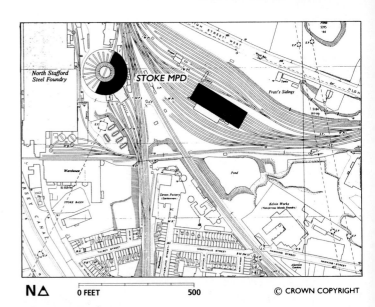

The collection of buildings forming the eight road straighthouse of **STOKE MPD** on May 1st, 1962.   *WT Stubbs Collection*

Map Dated: 1953
Site Location: South of the city centre, on the south side of High Street West (A50)
Track Status: Stoke Station and line are operational.

5F UTTOXETER

Location: In the middle of a triangle of lines, Uttoxeter Station forming two of the sides.(OS Map Ref: SK099333)

Directions: A cinder path leads to the shed from the eastern end of the eastbound platform on the Derby to Stoke line.

Closed: December 7th, 1964.

Description: A brick built 3TS dead ended shed.

Post Closure History: *Demolished.*

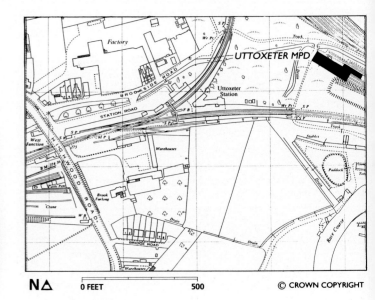

UTTOXETER MPD on April 15th, 1956.   *Dave Marriott*

Map Dated: 1964
Site Location: South east of town centre, on the east side of Highwood Road (B5017)
Track Status: Uttoxeter Station and line are operational.

17B BURTON

Location: On the west side of the line, south of Burton on Trent Station. (OS Map Ref: SK23702265)

Directions: Turn left outside the station along Borough Road, left into Wellington Street and left again into Shobnall Road. A cinder path leads to the shed from a gate on the right hand side, just before the bridge.

Closed: September 1966

Description: A brick built double roundhouse

Post Closure History: Most of the building still stands, in use as a timber store. A diesel depot (Code BU), now closed, stands in the shed yard. (1990)

BURTON MPD was a typical ex-MR roundhouse as can be seen in this general view, taken on September 30th, 1962.   *WT Stubbs Collection*

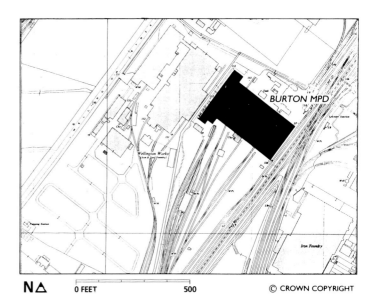

N△   0 FEET   500   © CROWN COPYRIGHT

Map Dated: 1952
Site Location: South of the town centre.
Track Status: Burton on Trent Station and line are operational.

Both the steam sheds in Burton on Trent are still standing, as is the 2TS Diesel Depot, built in the ex-MR shed yard and now abandoned.

17B(s) HORNINGLOW

Location: At the end of a goods spur off the main line, north of Burton Station. (OS Map Ref: SK251237)

Directions: Turn right outside the station along Borough Road, continue into Station Street, turn left into Guild Street, left at the end into Horninglow Street and right into Hawkins Lane. A path leads to the shed from a gate on the right hand side, on the railway bridge.

Closed: September 12th, 1960.

Description: A brick built 6TS dead ended shed.

Post Closure History: Still Standing. In use as a Transport Depot for Bass Charringtons, the roof has been rebuilt, but the walls remain intact. The whole railway site is now a huge storage area for beer kegs. (1990)

HORNINGLOW MPD just prior to nationalisation.
Bernard Matthews Collection

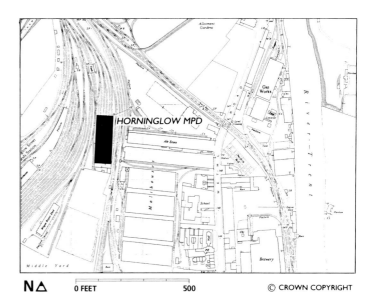

N△   0 FEET   500   © CROWN COPYRIGHT

Map Dated: 1953.
Site Location: North of the town centre, on the west bank of the River Trent.
Track Status: Burton Station and Derby line are operational. Goods spur and yards lifted.

LINCOLNSHIRE

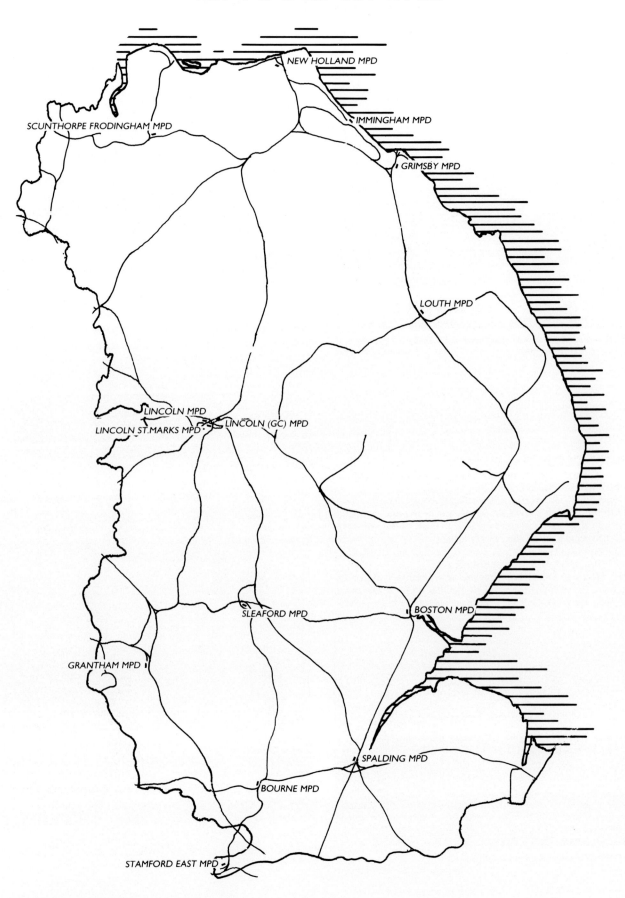

NEW HOLLAND MPD

IMMINGHAM MPD

GRIMSBY MPD

SCUNTHORPE FRODINGHAM MPD

LOUTH MPD

LINCOLN MPD

LINCOLN ST.MARKS MPD — LINCOLN (GC) MPD

SLEAFORD MPD

BOSTON MPD

GRANTHAM MPD

SPALDING MPD

BOURNE MPD

STAMFORD EAST MPD

40A LINCOLN

Location: South of the line, west of Lincoln Central Station. (OS Map Ref: SK972710)

Directions: Turn left outside of the station along St. Mary's Street, turn left into High Street, right into St. Mark's Lane and right into Brayford Wharf East. A footbridge on the left hand side crosses the waterway and leads to the shed.

Closed: January 1964.

Description: A brick built 4TS dead ended shed.

Post Closure History: *Still Standing, in a derelict condition (1990)*

LINCOLN MPD, packed full of ex-LNER locomotives on July 23rd, 1960.

Ken Fairey

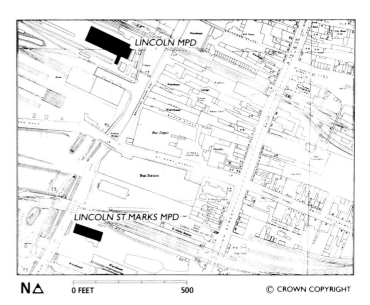

N △   0 FEET   500   © CROWN COPYRIGHT

Map Dated: 1971

Site Location: West of the town centre, on the west side of High Street (A15)

Track Status: Lincoln Central Station and line are operational. Lincoln St. Marks Station closed in 1985.

16A(s) LINCOLN ST. MARKS (MR)

Location: South of the line, at the west end of Lincoln (MR) Station. (OS Map Ref: SK972707)

Directions: Entrance to the shed is effected from the station platform.

Closed: January 1959

Description: A brick built 2TS through road shed.

Post Closure History: *Demolished*

LINCOLN ST.MARKS MPD, two years after closure, on June 4th, 1961. The buffer stops, visible on the other side of the shed building were strategically disposed to prevent itinerant locomotives from ending up in the River Witham which flowed within feet of the end of the building. The casual observer is left to ruminate why a through road, rather than a dead ended shed was built in the first place!

WT Stubbs Collection

MIDDLETON TOP

Illustration by Charles William Butterworth

40A(s) LINCOLN (GC)

Location: South of the Reepham line, east of Lincoln Central Station. (OS Map Ref: SK982708)

Directions: Turn right outside of the station into St. Mary's Street, proceed along Norman Place and ascend a flight of steps (after passing under a bridge) on the right and turn left at the top over the bridge. After crossing the railway descend the flight of steps on the left and cross the road at the bottom, continue along Great Northern Terrace and proceed across the level crossing. A boarded crossing leads to the shed from a gate on the left hand side.

Closed: May 1939 and subsequently used as stabling point, for steam locomotives, and Crew Depot until c1957.

Description: Originally a brick built 4TS dead ended shed by BR days the shed was roofless and used for rolling stock with the locos stabling in the yard.

Post Closure History: *Demolished in the mid-fifties.*

The substantially built **LINCOLN (GC) MPD** in LNER days.   *WA Camwell*

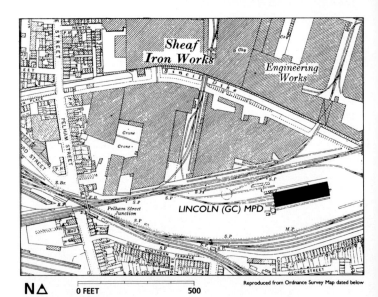

Map Dated: 1926

Site Location: East of the town centre, on the east side of Pelham Street.

Track Status: Line operational.

A purpose built Diesel Depot was erected alongside the original shed site and opened in 1956/7. The depot closed on October 4th, 1987 and is currently still standing, leased to RFS Industries Ltd, the owners of the former Doncaster Wagon Works.

35A(s) SPALDING

Location: West of the Bourne line, south of Spalding Station. (OS Map Ref: TF240221)

Directions: Leave the station by the approach road, turn right along Winsover Road, cross the level crossing and immediately turn left along St.John's Road. The shed entrance is a short distance along on the left hand side.

Closed: March 7th, 1960.

Description: A brick built 2TS dead ended shed.

Post Closure History: *Demolished (1965)*

Ex-GN locomotives at **SPALDING MPD** on October 12th, 1952.   *Ken Fairey*

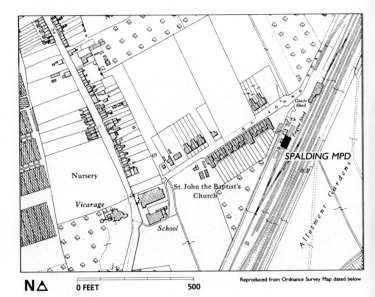

Map Dated: 1931

Site Location: West of the town centre, on the south side of Winsford Road (A151)

Track Status: Spalding Station and line are operational

35A(s) BOURNE

Location: On the west side of the line, south of Bourne Station. (OS Map Ref: TF095197)
Directions: Entrance to the shed is effected from the station platform.
Out of Use: 1953
Description: A brick built 2TS dead ended shed
Post Closure History: Demolished.

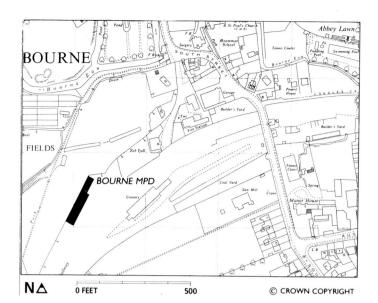

The abandoned shed building at **BOURNE MPD**, complete with weed-strewn yard, on August 28th, 1960.   *WT Stubbs Collection*

Map Dated: 1969 (Shed superimposed)
Site Location: South of the town centre, on the west side of South Road (A15)
Track Status: Bourne Station closed in 1959. Line lifted.

35A(s) STAMFORD EAST

Location: North of the line, east of Stamford (East) Station. (OS Map Ref: TF038071)
Directions: Entrance to the shed is effected from the station platform.
Closed: March 4th, 1957 (Line Closure Date)
Description: A brick built 1TS through road shed.
Post Closure History: Demolished. Site unused. (1990)

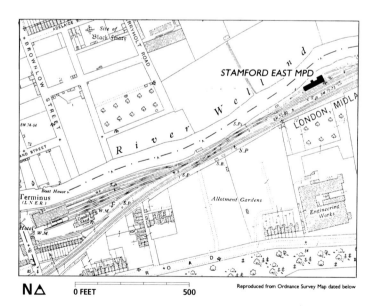

Ex-LNER Class C12 4–4–2T No. 67376 standing outside of **STAMFORD EAST MPD**. A typical branch line scene from the 1950s, now sadly just a fond memory.   *WT Stubbs Collection*

Map Dated: 1930
Site Location: On the east side of the town, on the south bank of the River Welland.
Track Status: Stamford (East) Station closed in 1957. Line lifted. Stamford Station and line are operational.

35B GRANTHAM

Location: On the west side of Grantham Station. (OS Map Ref: SK914350)
Directions: Turn left outside of the station, into Station Road and left into a subway leading under the railway. The shed entrance is on the left hand side at the end of this subway.
Closed: September 1963.
Description: A 4TS dead ended brick built 'new' shed and a 4TS brick built 'old' shed with 2 through roads.
Post Closure History: Demolished. Site unused.

The 'new' shed at **GRANTHAM MPD** on May 16th, 1963.   *Ken Fairey*

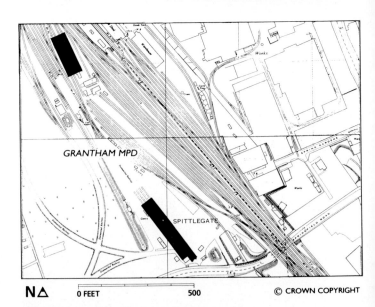

N△   0 FEET   500   © CROWN COPYRIGHT

Map Dated: 1965 ('Old' Shed Superimposed)
Site Location: South of the town centre, on the north side of Springfield Road (B677)
Track Status: Grantham Station and line are operational.
The northernmost building is the 'old' shed. The turning triangle on the left hand side of the shed site incorporated a scissors crossing and was unique on BR.

36C FRODINGHAM (SCUNTHORPE)

Location: North of the line, east of Scunthorpe Station. (OS Map Ref: SE905115)
Directions: Turn right outside of the station into Station Road, turn fifth left into Cole Street, turn right into High Street and bear left into Dawes Lane. The shed entrance is on the right hand side, some distance along this lane.
Closed: February 26th, 1966 (Steam)
Description: A concrete built 5TS through road shed.
Post Closure History: Demolished. The site is now occupied by a purpose built diesel depot (Code FH). (1988)

Two things you could always guarantee about **FRODINGHAM (SCUN-THORPE) MPD** in BR days were that you would always find it packed with ex-LNER O1 & O4 and WD 2–8–0 locomotives, and that you would hardly be able to see them for smoke and grime. A typical line up, viewed on May 26th, 1963.
Ken Fairey

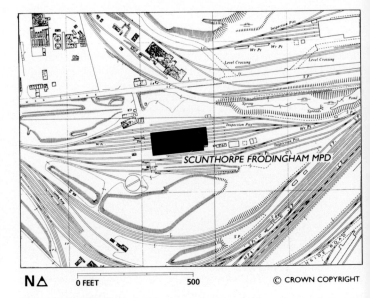

N△   0 FEET   500   © CROWN COPYRIGHT

Map Dated: 1965
Site Location: North of the town centre, on the east side of the A1077.
Track Status: Scunthorpe Station and line are operational.

40B IMMINGHAM

Location: In Immingham Docks. (OS Map Ref: TA199151)

Directions: Turn right outside of Immingham Dock Station and follow the Dock Road around the perimeter of the west and south sides of the dock. Bear right towards the Dock Entrance nearest to Immingham Village and the shed entrance is on the right.

Closed: February 1966 (Steam)

Description: A brick built 11TS through road shed.

Post Closure History: Part of the steam shed buildings remain, as does the coaling tower, whilst a purpose built diesel depot occupies the rest of the site (Code IM) (1988).

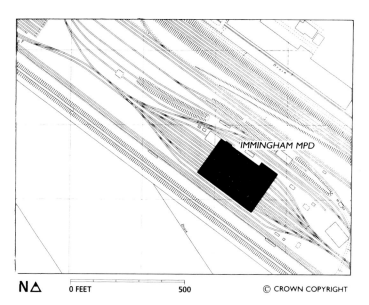

© CROWN COPYRIGHT

Map Dated: 1964

Site Location: North-east of Immingham town centre, on the east side of the A1136.

Track Status: Lines operational.

The uniquely profiled roof of **IMMINGHAM MPD** is clearly shown in this view of the shed and yard on November 7th, 1962. *Ken Fairey*

40B(s) NEW HOLLAND

Location: On the south side of the New Holland to New Holland Town to Barton on Humber triangle of lines, at the south end of New Holland Town Station. (OS Map Ref: TA082242)

Directions: Entrance to the shed is effected from the level crossing at the south end of New Holland Town Station approach road.

Closed: April 1941 and subsequently used as a Stabling Point until c1960.

Description: A brick built 4TS through road shed.

Post Closure History: Demolished. Site unused. (1974)

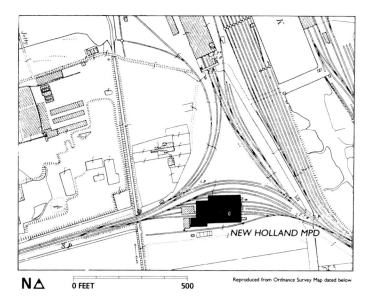

Reproduced from Ordnance Survey Map dated below

Map Dated: 1902

Site Location: North of the town centre, on the west side of the B1206.

Track Status: New Holland Town Station closed in 1983. Some lines operational.

NEW HOLLAND MPD in June 1952. Despite pre-BR closure the building and yard lingered on in use as a Stabling Point into the 1960s, the precise date of abandonment uncertain. *Allan Sommerfield Collection*

40B(s) GRIMSBY

Location: On the east side of the line, north of Grimsby Town Station. (OS Map Ref: TA275102)

Directions: Cross the station yard and proceed into Corn Place, turn right along Victoria Street and continue into Victoria Street North. Turn right into Market Street, cross the railway by means of the footbridge and turn left at the end along Railway Street. The shed entrance is on the left hand side along this street.

Closed: 1912, and subsequently used as a Stabling Point for dock shunters until about 1961.

Description: Originally a brick built 6TS dead ended shed, by 1948 totally roofless.

Post Closure History: Demolished by 1962, the track is still in situ, with the pits filled in, and is used by coal wagons for the local Coal Merchant.

Early design Diesel Shunters including Barclay 0–6–0 No. 11180 sit inside the shell of the former shed building at **GRIMSBY MPD** on August 17th, 1958.
WT Stubbs Collection

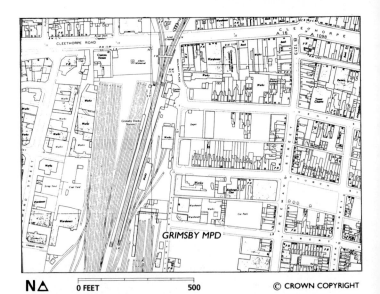

N△   0 FEET   500   © CROWN COPYRIGHT

Map Dated: 1964

Site Location: North east of the town centre, on the south side of Cleethorpe Road (A16)

Track Status: Grimsby Town Station and line are operational
Following closure in 1912, three roads were de-roofed and used for stabling dock shunters, the other portion retained its roof and was used for wagon repairs.

40C LOUTH

Location: Adjacent to the east side of Louth Station. (OS Map Ref: TF333879)

Directions: Entrance to the shed is effected from the station platform.

Closed: December 1956.

Description: A brick built 2TS through road shed.

Post Closure History: Demolished. Site unused. (1987)

An early BR view of the small ex-GN shed at **LOUTH MPD**, built alongside the station platform and the delightfully poetic 'Louth South' Signal Box.
Allan Sommerfield Collection

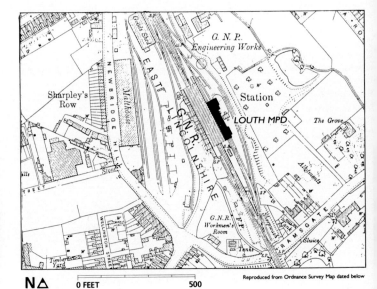

N△   0 FEET   500   Reproduced from Ordnance Survey Map dated below

Map Dated: 1908

Site Location: North of the town centre, On the north side of Ramsgate Road.

Track Status: Louth Station closed in 1970. Line lifted.

40F BOSTON

Location: On the west side of the line, south of Boston Station. (OS Map Ref: TF322435)

Directions: Turn right outside of the station into the approach road, left into West Street, right into Queen Street and right into Broadfield Street. A level crossing leads to the shed from the end of this street.

Closed: January 6th, 1964

Description: A brick built 9TS dead ended shed

Post Closure History: *Demolished.*

Ex-LNER Class B1 4–6–0 No. 61114 stands amongst a large collection of ex-LMS Class 4 2–6–0 locomotives at **BOSTON MPD** on November 12th, 1961.

Ken Fairey

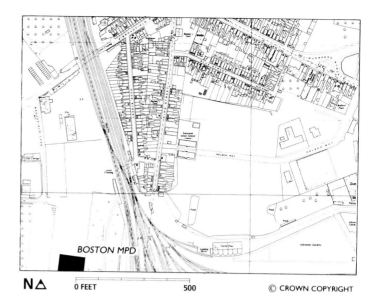

N△ 0 FEET 500 © CROWN COPYRIGHT

Map Dated: 1968 (Shed superimposed)

Site Location: South of the town centre, on the west side of the A16.

Track Status: Boston Station and line are operational.

40F(s) SLEAFORD

Location: South of the Grantham to Boston line, west of Sleaford Station. (OS Map Ref: TF065454)

Directions: Turn right outside of the station into the approach road and right over the level crossing. Bear right into Grantham Road and a gate on the right hand side leads to the shed through the goods yard.

Closed: May 1964.

Description: A brick built 2TS dead ended shed.

Post Closure History: *Demolished. Site in use for commercial development.*

SLEAFORD MPD in BR days.

WT Stubbs Collection

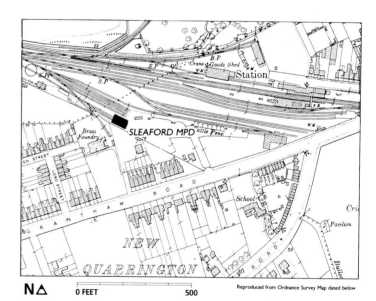

N△ 0 FEET 500 Reproduced from Ordnance Survey Map dated below

Map Dated: 1905

Site Location: West of the town centre, on the north side of the A153.

Track Status: Sleaford Station and line are operational.

PART ELEVEN

LANCASHIRE

MANCHESTER LIVERPOOL LANCASHIRE

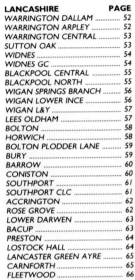

ACCRINGTON MPD *(WT Stubbs)*

LANCASHIRE

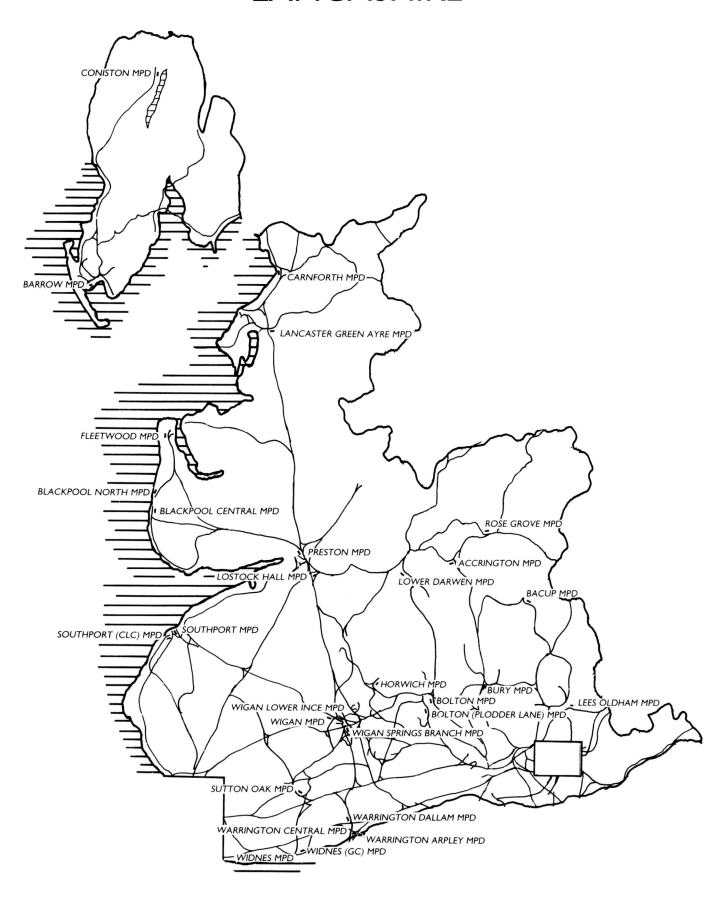

CONISTON MPD

BARROW MPD

CARNFORTH MPD

LANCASTER GREEN AYRE MPD

FLEETWOOD MPD

BLACKPOOL NORTH MPD

BLACKPOOL CENTRAL MPD

ROSE GROVE MPD

PRESTON MPD

ACCRINGTON MPD

LOWER DARWEN MPD

LOSTOCK HALL MPD

BACUP MPD

SOUTHPORT (CLC) MPD — SOUTHPORT MPD

HORWICH MPD

BURY MPD

WIGAN LOWER INCE MPD

BOLTON MPD

LEES OLDHAM MPD

WIGAN MPD

BOLTON (PLODDER LANE) MPD

WIGAN SPRINGS BRANCH MPD

SUTTON OAK MPD

WARRINGTON DALLAM MPD

WARRINGTON CENTRAL MPD

WARRINGTON ARPLEY MPD

WIDNES MPD   WIDNES (GC) MPD

8B WARRINGTON DALLAM

Location: On the west side of the West Coast Main Line, about 1 mile north of Warrington Bank Quay Station. (OS Map Ref: SJ602894)

Directions: Turn left outside of the station along Parker Street, right into Sankey Street, left into Horsemarket Street and proceed along Winwick Street, continuing into Winwick Road. Turn left into Kerfoot Street and bear right over the bridge into Folly Lane. The shed entrance is on the left, just past the bridge.

Closed: October 2nd, 1967.

Description: A brick built 10TS dead ended shed.

Post Closure History: Still Standing. In Industrial use. (1990)

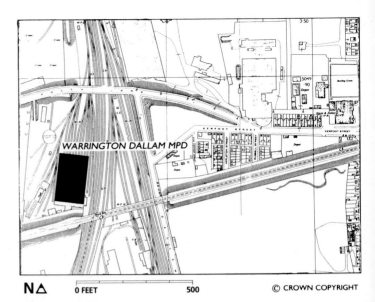

Stanier locomotives monopolise the shed yard at **WARRINGTON DALLAM MPD** on July 17th, 1955.
Bill Potter

Map Dated: 1963

Site Location: North of the town centre, on the west side of Winwick Road (A49)

Track Status: Warrington Bank Quay Station and line are operational.

8B(s) WARRINGTON ARPLEY

Location: On the south side of Warrington Arpley Station. (OS Map Ref: SJ605877)

Directions: Turn right outside of the station and first right into a narrow road running alongside a canal. A door on the right hand side, just past the bridge leads to the shed.

Closed: May 27th, 1963.

Description: A brick built 2TS through road shed, latterly roofless.

Post Closure History: Demolished. Shed roads used for stabling diesel locomotives. (1990)

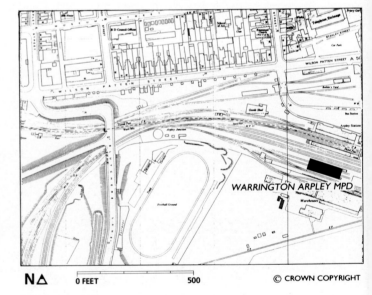

The roofless shed building at **WARRINGTON ARPLEY MPD** on April 2nd, 1961.
Hugh Ballantyne

Map Dated: 1964

Site Location: South of the town centre, on the north bank of the River Mersey.

Track Status: Arpley Station closed in 1958. Line operational.

13E(s) WARRINGTON CENTRAL

Location: On the south side of Warrington Central Station. (OS Map Ref: SJ607885)

Directions: Entrance to the shed is effected from the station platform.

Out of Use: 1966

Description: Consisting of an Engine Pit only. There are no shed buildings.

Post Closure History: *Lines lifted.*

An ex-LMS Class 4F 0–6–0 stands alongside the basic facilities at **WARRINGTON CENTRAL MPD** on August 14th, 1960. *WT Stubbs Collection*

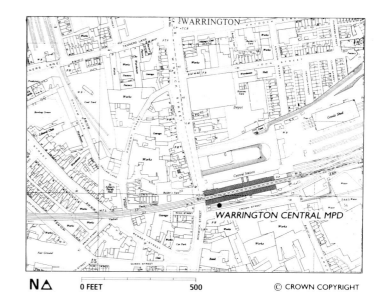

Map Dated: 1963

Site Location: In the town centre, on the east side of Winwick Street (A49)

Track Status: Warrington Central Station and line are operational.

10E SUTTON OAK

Location: East of the line, between Sutton Oak and Peasley Cross Stations. (OS Map Ref: SJ527941)

Directions: Turn left outside of Peasley Cross Station along Sutton Road, turn right into Baxters Lane and the shed entrance is on the right hand side.

Closed: June 19th, 1967.

Description: A brick built 10TS dead ended shed.

Post Closure History: *Still Standing. The building is in use as a supermarket and the shed yard is now a Car Park. (1990)*

Ex-LMS Class 4F 0–6–0s Nos 44497 and 44066 stand in the shed yard at **SUTTON OAK MPD** on September 24th, 1961. *Ken Fairey*

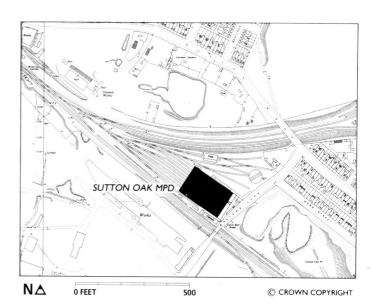

Map Dated: 1958

Site Location: East of St.Helens town centre, on the east side of the A570.

Track Status: Sutton Oak Station closed in 1951. Line operational.

8D WIDNES

Location: In the fork of the Widnes South to Warrington and St.Helens lines. (OS Map Ref: SJ515849)

Directions: Turn right outside of the station along Victoria Street, right into Croft Street and after about 200 yards turn right into a short cul-de-sac. The shed entrance is on the left hand side.

Closed: April 13th, 1964.

Description: A brick built 6TS dead ended shed.

Post Closure History: Demolished. Site unused. (1990)

WIDNES MPD on September 10th, 1961.   *WT Stubbs Collection*

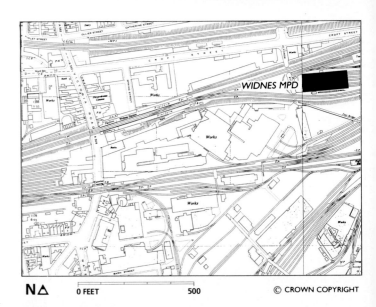

Map Dated: 1959

Site Location: South of the town centre, on the east side of Victoria Road (A568)

Track Status: Widnes South Station closed in 1962. Line lifted.

13E(s) WIDNES (GC)

Location: North of the line, west of Tanhouse Lane Station. (OS Map Ref: SJ526853)

Directions: Entrance to the shed is effected from the level crossing at the western end of the station.

Closed: 1956

Description: A brick built 2TS dead ended shed.

Post Closure History: Demolished.

A pre-war view of LMS 'Jinty' 0–6–0T No. 7464 *(Later BR No. 47464)* standing outside of **WIDNES (GC) MPD**. Although officially listed as 'GC' it was jointly owned and operated by both GC and MR, and of course subsequently by LNER and LMS.   *Bernard Matthews Collection*

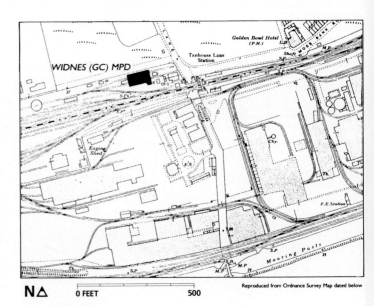

Reproduced from Ordnance Survey Map dated below

Map Dated: 1937

Site Location: East of the town centre, on the west side of Tanhouse Lane.

Track Status: Tanhouse Lane Station closed in 1964. Line lifted.

28A BLACKPOOL CENTRAL

Location: On the east side of the line, south of Blackpool Central Station. (OS Map Ref: SD310350)

Directions: Turn left outside the station and left again along the promenade. After some distance, turn left into Rigby Road and the shed entrance is on the right hand side, just past the bridge.

Closed: November 2nd, 1964.

Description: A brick built 8TS dead ended shed

Post Closure History: Demolished. The entire site is in use as a coach and car park. (1990)

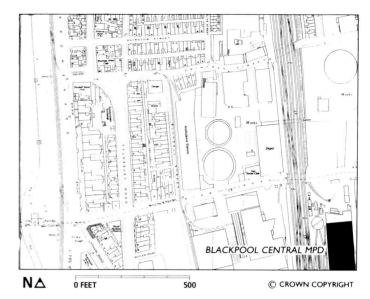

Map Dated: 1963

Site Location: South of the town centre, on the south side of Rigby Road.

Track Status: Blackpool Central Station closed in 1964. Line lifted.

The large depot at **BLACKPOOL CENTRAL MPD** plays host to a visiting ex-LNER Class B1 4–6–0 on June 11th, 1962. *WT Stubbs Collection*

28A(s) BLACKPOOL NORTH

Location: On the north side of the line, east of Blackpool North Station. (OS Map Ref: SD311371)

Directions: Turn right outside the station and first right into Queen Street. Turn left into High Street, right into Pleasant Street and bear left at the end, turning right into Ashburton Road. A path between two blocks of houses on the right hand side leads to the shed.

Closed: February 10th, 1964.

Description: A brick built 3TS dead ended shed.

Post Closure History: Demolished

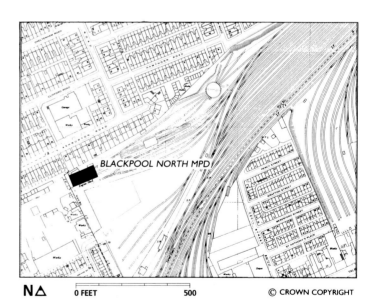

Map Dated: 1963

Site Location: North of the town centre, on the east side of Egerton Road.

Track Status: Blackpool North Station and line are operational.

Ex-LMS Jubilee Class 4–6–0 No. 45571 *SOUTH AFRICA* stands alongside the shed building at **BLACKPOOL NORTH MPD** on September 6th, 1962. *Ken Fairey*

10A SPRINGS BRANCH (WIGAN)

Location: East of the main line, about a mile south of Wigan North Western Station. (OS Map Ref: SD593038)

Directions: Turn right outside of the station into Wallgate, right into King Street, proceed along Darlington Street and turn right into Warrington Lane. Continue along Warrington Road for about a mile and turn right into Morris Street. The shed entrance is at the end of this cul-de-sac.

Closed: December 4th, 1967.

Description: A depot complex consisting of two brick built 6TS dead ended sheds.

Post Closure History: *No.2 Shed was demolished and replaced by a purpose built Diesel Depot (Code SP), whilst No.1 was retained for Stores. The whole site has since been demolished and diesel locomotives now stable on the site. (1990)*

Ex-LNWR designs were well represented at **WIGAN SPRINGS BRANCH MPD** when viewed on September 10th, 1961. *WT Stubbs*

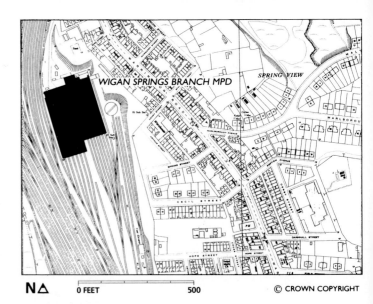

Map Dated: 1954

Site Location: South of the town centre, on the west side of Warrington Road (A573)

Track Status: Wigan North Western Station and line are operational.

13G WIGAN LOWER INCE

Location: West of the line, at the south end of Wigan Central Station. (OS Map Ref: SD591049)

Directions: Turn left outside Wigan (ex-LNER) Station into Station Road, continue into Chapel Lane, turn left into Darlington Street and turn right into Warrington Lane. Turn left into Railway Street and the shed entrance is at the end.

Closed: March 24th, 1952.

Description: A brick built 2TS through road shed.

Post Closure History: *Demolished. Site occupied by 'Arctic Freezer Centre' (1990)*

LNER Class J10 0–6–0 No. 5123 *(Later BR No. 65197)* standing outside of **WIGAN LOWER INCE MPD** on an April day in 1939. *Allan Sommerfield Collection*

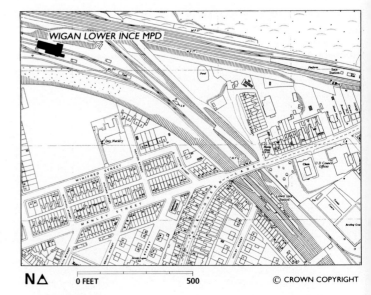

Map Dated: 1954

Site Location: South east of the town centre, on the east side of Warrington Road (A573)

Track Status: Wigan Central Station closed in 1964. Line lifted.

27D WIGAN (L&Y)

Location: South of the Southport line, west of Wigan Wallgate Station. (OS Map Ref: SD575057)

Directions: Turn right outside of Wigan North Western Station along Wallgate, left into King Street West, bear left into Dorning Street and turn left into Frog Lane. Turn left into Prescott Street, right into Cricket Street and the shed entrance is a door at the end of this short street.

Closed: April 13th, 1964.

Description: A brick and timber built 14TS dead ended shed, latterly reduced to an 8TS structure.

Post Closure History: Demolished. Site of commercial development. (1988)

Ex-L&Y locomotives had all but been wiped out when this photograph of the former L&YR stronghold of **WIGAN MPD** was taken on September 24th, 1961, with former MR and LMS designs dominating the shed yard.   *Ken Fairey*

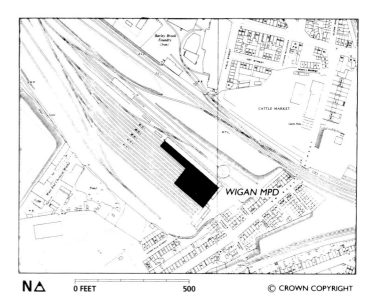

N△   0 FEET   500   © CROWN COPYRIGHT

Map Dated: 1955

Site Location: West of the town centre, on the south side of Frog Lane (B5375).

Track Status: Wigan Wallgate Station and line are operational.

26F LEES (OLDHAM)

Location: On the north side of Lees Station. (OS Map Ref: SK579029)

Directions: Turn right outside the station into St. John Street and a cinder path on the right hand side, just past the bridge leads to the shed.

Closed: April 13th, 1964.

Description: A brick built 6TS dead ended shed. (Rebuilt in 1955).

Post Closure History: Demolished. The whole site is now a housing estate. (1990)

The rebuilt **LEES OLDHAM MPD** on May 15th, 1960.   *Ken Fairey*

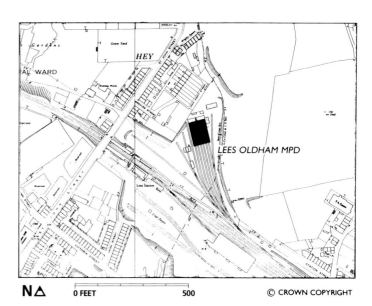

N△   0 FEET   500   © CROWN COPYRIGHT

Map Dated: 1954

Site Location: East of Oldham town centre, on the north side of Oldham Road (A669)

Track Status: Lees Station closed in 1955. Lines lifted.

26C BOLTON

Location: On the west side of the Bolton Trinity Street to Clifton Junction line, south of the station. (OS Map Ref: SD725075)
Directions: Turn left outside of Bolton Trinity Street Station into Trinity Street, left again into Station Street and proceed along Montcrieffe Street. Turn right into Lever Street, left into Nelson Street and continue into Crescent Road. Turn left along Back Dobie Street and the shed entrance is opposite the end of this short street.
Closed: July 1st, 1968.
Description: A brick built 12TS dead ended shed.
Post Closure History: Demolished

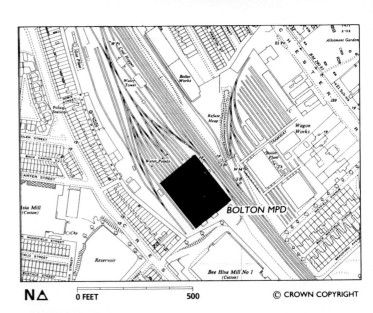

N△ 0 FEET 500 © CROWN COPYRIGHT

Map Dated: 1951
Site Location: South of the town centre, on the west side of Manchester Road (A666)
Track Status: Bolton Station and line are operational.

BOLTON MPD on August 16th, 1959. *WT Stubbs Collection*

26C(s) HORWICH

Location: In the Horwich Works complex on the south side of the Horwich Branch, midway between Blackrod and Horwich Stations. (OS Map Ref: SD637109)
Directions: Leave Horwich Station and go straight ahead into Drinkwater Lane, turn right at the end into Chorley New Road and the works entrance is on the left hand side.
Closed: April 17th, 1948.
Description: There are no shed buildings. The allocation, a rail motor, stabled within the works complex.
Post Closure History: Following the elimination of steam locomotives the main activity of the works until closure was the repair of wagons and EMUs. The buildings are now in use as Industrial Units. (1990)

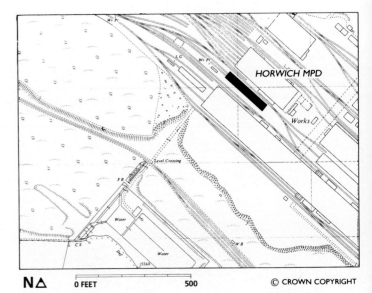

N△ 0 FEET 500 © CROWN COPYRIGHT

Map Dated: 1961.
Site Location: South of the town, on the west side of the A673.
Track Status: Horwich Station closed in 1965.
The ex-L&YR Rail Motor No. 50617 was employed on the Horwich branch and stabled within the works. The 'stabling point' became redundant upon withdrawal of the unit on April 17th, 1948.

The Works Shunter servicing & stabling area and, on the right hand side, 2TS shed at **HORWICH MPD** on June 17th, 1962. *WT Stubbs Collection*

10D BOLTON (PLODDER LANE)

Location: On the west side of the line, north of Plodder Lane Station. (OS Map Ref: SD719062)

Directions: A cinder path runs parallel to the line from the opposite side of the road to the station entrance.

Closed: October 10th, 1954.

Description: A brick built 6TS dead ended shed.

Post Closure History: Demolished. Now site of housing estate. (1990)

BOLTON PLODDER LANE MPD on August 9th, 1953.
Bernard Matthews Collection

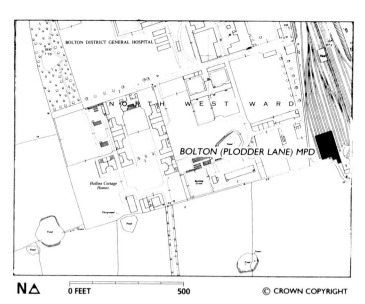

N △   0 FEET   500   © CROWN COPYRIGHT

Map Dated: 1952

Site Location: South of the town centre, on the north side of Plodder Lane.

Track Status: Plodder Lane Station closed in 1954. Line lifted.

26D BURY

Location: On the east side of the Bury (Bolton Street) to Radcliffe line, south of Bury (Bolton Street) Station. (OS Map Ref: SD799102)

Directions: Turn left outside of Bury Knowsley Street Station along Knowsley Street and right into Baron Street. The shed entrance is on the left hand side.

Closed: April 12th, 1965. (Steam)

Description: A brick built 8TS dead ended shed.

Post Closure History: Demolished. Used for electric locomotive storage in the immediate years following closure to steam.

The closed shed at **BURY MPD** playing host to a sundry collection of diesel and electric locomotives in 1969.   *WT Stubbs Collection*

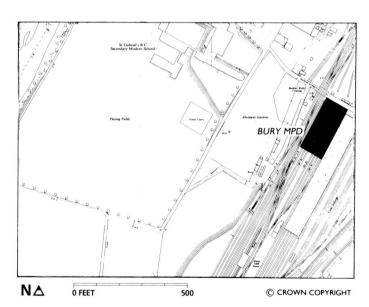

N △   0 FEET   500   © CROWN COPYRIGHT

Map Dated: 1958

Site Location: South of the town centre, on the west side of Manchester Road (A56)

Track Status: Bury Bolton Street Station is closed, having been replaced by a new Interchange station. Line operational.

11B BARROW

Location: On the south side of the old Furness Railway Works, adjacent to Barrow Docks. (OS Map Ref: SD206685)

Directions: Cross the yard outside of Barrow Station and turn left across Abbey Road into Rawlinson Street. Proceed along for about one mile and turn right at the end into Salthouse Road. A path leads through the old works to the shed from a lodge gate on the left hand side.

Closed: December 12th, 1966. (Steam)

Description: A brick built 10TS dead ended shed.

Post Closure History: Demolished. Site unused. (1987)

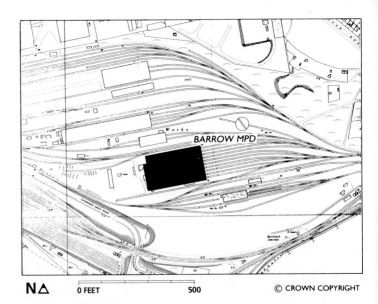

N△   0 FEET   500   © CROWN COPYRIGHT

Map Dated: 1958

Site Location: South east of the town centre, on the north side of Cavendish Dock Road.

Track Status: Most lines lifted.

The shed remained in use as a Diesel Depot (Code BW) until 1977

With the dockyard cranes in the background and a MetroVick Co–Bo in the yard this unique scene can only be at **BARROW MPD**. The view was taken on May 9th, 1965 and shows the dwindling steam allocation slowly being ousted by DMUs and diesel locomotives.
WT Stubbs Collection

11B(s) CONISTON

Location: On the east side of the line, south of Coniston Lake Station. (OS Map Ref: SD301974)

Directions: Entrance to the shed is effected from the station platform. (From the Village Centre: Follow the A593 to Broughton and turn right up Station Road, just past a petrol station, and the station drive is second on the left)

Closed: January 1958.

Description: A stone built 1TS through road shed.

Post Closure History: Demolished. The whole site has been redeveloped as a small housing and business estate. (1990)

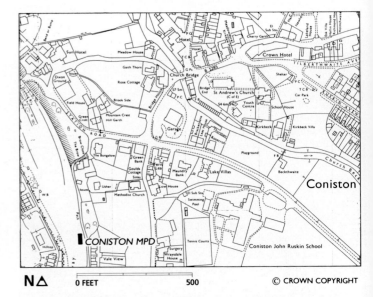

N△   0 FEET   500   © CROWN COPYRIGHT

Map Dated: 1977 (Shed superimposed)

Site Location: South of the village centre, on the east side of the A593)

Track Status: Coniston Station closed in 1958. Line lifted.

The abandoned and isolated shed at **CONISTON MPD** on June 26th, 1963.
WT Stubbs Collection

27C SOUTHPORT

Location: North of the line, east of Southport Chapel Street Station. (OS Map Ref: SD342170)

Directions: Turn right outside of the station into Chapel Street, first right into London Street, left into Derby Road and the goods yard entrance is on the right hand side. A path leads through this yard to the shed.

Closed: June 6th, 1966.

Description: A brick built 6TS dead ended shed.

Post Closure History: *Still Standing. Preserved as headquarters of the Steamport Preservation Group. (1989)*

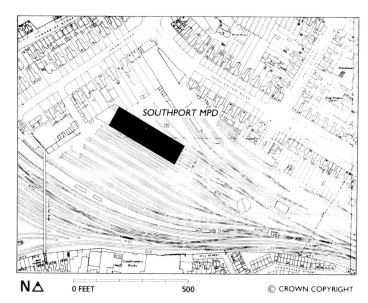

SOUTHPORT MPD on July 21st, 1963   *WT Stubbs Collection*

Map Dated: 1965

Site Location: In the town centre, on the south side of Kensington Road

Track Status: Southport Station and line are operational

13E(s) SOUTHPORT (CLC)

Location: West of the line, at the north end of Southport (Lord Street) Station. (OS Map Ref: SD329171)

Directions: Entrance to the shed is effected from the station yard.

Closed: July 7th, 1952

Description: A brick built 2TS dead ended shed.

Post Closure History: *Demolished. Site unused. (1988)*

The obscure **SOUTHPORT (CLC) MPD** in early BR days.
Allan Sommerfield Collection

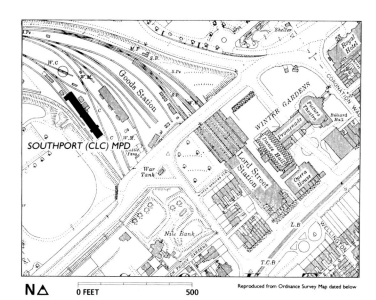

Map Dated: 1928

Site Location: Adjacent to the sea front on the north side of Rotten Row.

Track Status: Southport (Lord Street) Station closed in 1952. Line lifted.

24A ACCRINGTON

Location: On the south side of the line, between Accrington and Church & Oswaldtwistle Stations. (OS Map Ref: SD747283)

Directions: Go straight ahead outside Accrington Station along the approach road and turn left into Eagle Street. Turn left into Blackburn Road, left again into Willows Lane and then right into Charter Street. The shed entrance is on the right hand side.

Closed: March 6th, 1961 (Steam)

Description: Originally an 8TS brick built dead ended shed, it had been reduced to a 6TS building by BR days.

Post Closure History: *Following closure to steam became a DMU depot. Since closed completely and demolished.*

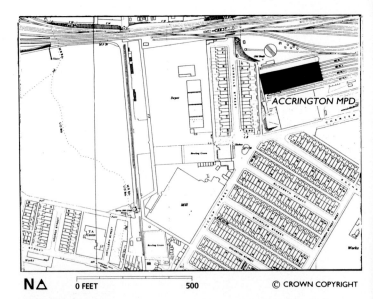

A few tank engines occupy the shed yard at **ACCRINGTON MPD** on May 21st, 1960.
Ken Fairey

Map Dated: 1958
Site Location: In the west of the town, south of the A679
Track Status: Accrington Station and line are operational.

24B ROSE GROVE

Location: North of the line, west of Rose Grove Station. (OS Map Ref: SD811322)

Directions: Turn right outside of the station and first left along Rose Grove Lane. The shed entrance is on the left hand side.

Closed: August 5th, 1968.

Description: A brick built 6TS dead ended shed.

Post Closure History: *Demolished. Most of the site is buried under the M65 Motorway.*

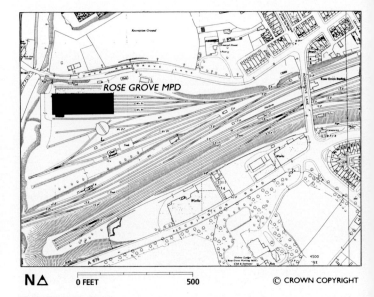

ROSE GROVE MPD on a wet and windy September 10th, 1961.
WT Stubbs Collection

Map Dated: 1960.
Site Location: West of Burnley, on the north side of Accrington Road (A679)
Track Status: Rose Grove Station and line are operational.

24D LOWER DARWEN

Location: West of the Darwen line, about 1.5 miles south of Blackburn Station. (OS Map Ref: SD682256)

Directions: Cross the yard outside of the station into Jubilee Street, turn left into Darwen Street, fork right into Great Bolton Street and proceed along Bolton Road for about 1.5 miles. This is the main Blackburn to Darwen Road (A666) and a footpath on the left hand side, opposite The Fernhurst Hotel leads across some fields and up a bank to the shed.

Closed: February 14th, 1966.

Description: A brick built 8TS dead ended shed.

***Post Closure History**: Demolished. Site unused. (1989)*

The ex-L&YR establishment, **LOWER DARWEN MPD** on September 10th, 1961.
WT Stubbs Collection

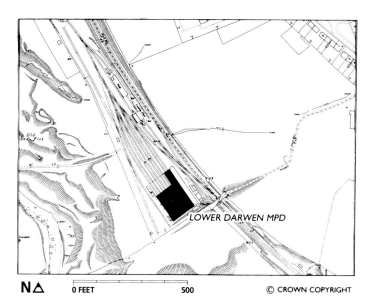

N△　0 FEET　500　© CROWN COPYRIGHT

Map Dated: 1955

Site Location: South of Blackburn town centre, on the east side of the A666.

Track Status: Line operational.

26E BACUP

Location: On the east side of the Rochdale line, south of Bacup Station. (OS Map Ref: SD873219)

Directions: Turn right outside the station into Rockliffe Road, and right at the end into Rochdale Road. Continue for about 800 yards and a path down a bank leads to the shed, from the right hand side of the road.

Closed: October 10th, 1954.

Description: A stone built 4TS through road shed.

***Post Closure History**: Demolished.*

An early BR scene with ex-LMS Class 4MT 2–6–4T No. 42287 and Class 7F 0–8–0 No. 49560 simmering in the shed yard at **BACUP MPD** on October 5th, 1951.
Bernard Matthews Collection

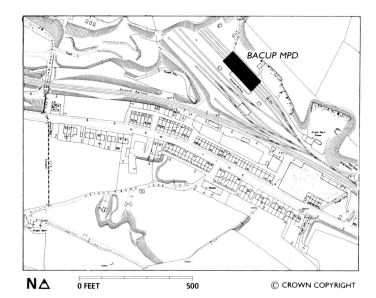

N△　0 FEET　500　© CROWN COPYRIGHT

Map Dated: 1964

Site Location: East of Bacup on the south side of Rochdale Road (A671)

Track Status: Bacup Station closed in 1966. Lines lifted.

10B PRESTON

Location: West of the main line, north of Preston Station. (OS Map Ref: SD531297)

Directions: Turn left outside of the station along Fishergate, right into Bow Lane, left into Marsh Lane and right into Croft Street. A path leads to the shed from the right hand side, just before the end of this street.

Closed: September 12th, 1961.

Description: A brick built 9TS dead ended shed.

Post Closure History: Demolished. Part of the shed site is occupied by a power signalbox. (1989)

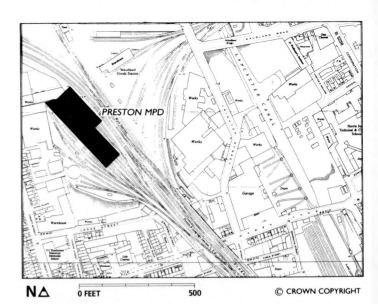

A variety of ex-LMS and BR Standard locomotives park in the remains of the roofless **PRESTON MPD** on August 13th, 1960, just over a month after the fire.

Ken Fairey

N△   0 FEET   500   © CROWN COPYRIGHT

Map Dated: 1960
Site Location: West of the town centre, on the north side of Marsh Lane
Track Status: Preston Station and line are operational.
The shed roof was extensively damaged by fire on June 27th, 1960.

24C LOSTOCK HALL

Location: On the south side of Lostock Hall Station. (OS Map Ref: SD682256)

Directions: Turn right outside of the station into Watkin Lane and the shed entrance is on the right hand side.

Closed: August 5th, 1968.

Description: A brick built 8TS dead ended shed.

Post Closure History: After closure was taken over and used by a BR Engineering Department until 1988. Demolished in January 1990.

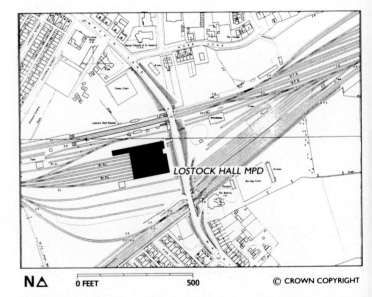

The last year of BR steam, and the locomotive stock had dwindled exclusively to Stanier designs at **LOSTOCK HALL MPD** when photographed on March 16th, 1968.

Alec Swain

N△   0 FEET   500   © CROWN COPYRIGHT

Map Dated: 1965
Site Location: South of Preston town centre, on the west side of Watkin Lane (A582)
Track Status: Lostock Hall Station and line are operational.

23C LANCASTER GREEN AYRE

Location: East of the line, south of Lancaster Green Ayre Station. (OS Map Ref: SD478620)

Directions: Leave the station along the approach road, turn right into Parliament Street, bear right into Cable Street and the shed entrance is on the right hand side.

Closed: April 18th, 1966.

Description: A brick built 4TS dead ended shed with all the roads diverging from a turntable, in similar fashion to a semi-roundhouse.

Post Closure History: *Demolished. The site is now occupied by a supermarket (1990)*

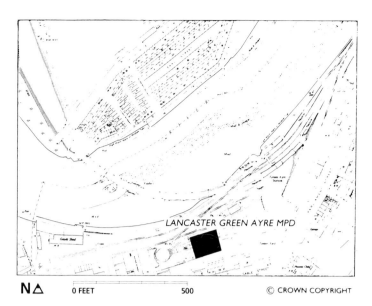

N △   0 FEET   500   © CROWN COPYRIGHT

Map Dated: 1957

Site Location: North of the town centre, on the south bank of the River Lune

Track Status: Lancaster Green Ayre Station closed in 1966. Line lifted.

Turntable breakdowns must have been a recurring nightmare to the staff at **LANCASTER GREEN AYRE MPD**. This view of the shed, taken on September 5th, 1962, clearly illustrates the confined layout of the depot.   *Ken Fairey*

11A CARNFORTH

Location: On the west side of the Barrow line, north west of Carnforth Station. (OS Map Ref: SD496708)

Directions: Turn left outside the station into Warton Road and after about 150 yards left again over a footbridge. This leads to the shed.

Closed: August 4th, 1968.

Description: A brick built 6TS through road shed.

Post Closure History: *Still Standing. Preserved as Steamtown Railway Museum. (1990)*

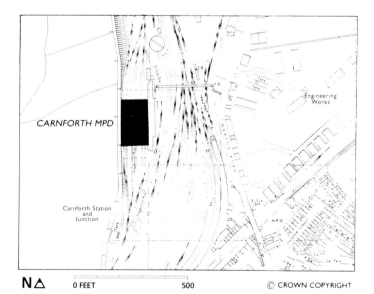

N △   0 FEET   500   © CROWN COPYRIGHT

Map Dated: 1970

Site Location: In the town centre.

Track Status: Carnforth Station and lines are operational.

CARNFORTH MPD, in BR days, on June 19th, 1961.   *WT Stubbs Collection*

28B FLEETWOOD

Location: West of the line, about a mile south of Fleetwood Station. (OS Map Ref: SD327465)

Directions: Turn left outside the station along Queens Terrace, continue into Dock Street and turn right into Station Road. Turn left into Radcliffe Road and the shed entrance is on the left hand side some distance along, opposite Heathfield Road.

Closed: February 14th, 1966

Description: A brick built 6TS dead ended shed.

Post Closure History: Still Standing. In industrial use (1988).

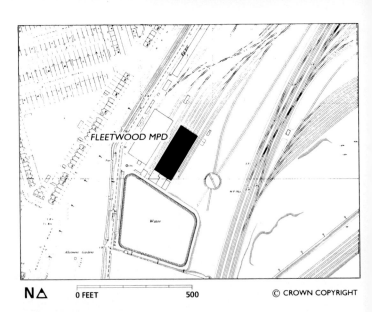

N△　　0 FEET　　　　　　500　　　　© CROWN COPYRIGHT

Map Dated: 1960

Site Location: In the north of the town, on the east side of Radcliffe Road.

Track Status: Fleetwood Station closed in 1970. Line lifted.

FLEETWOOD MPD on June 10th, 1962.　　　*WT Stubbs Collection*

Ex-LNER Class A4 4–6–2 No. 60019 *BITTERN* in store, awaiting preservation, in the roundhouse at **YORK NORTH MPD** on June 25th, 1968. This part of the depot became the premises for the National Railway Museum and was, until 1990, believed to be the last remaining double-roundhouse steam shed still in existence. The decision by the Museum to remove one of the turntables, effectively as an economy measure from what they classify as an Industrial Building! *(sic)*, remains one of the most short sighted pieces of professional vandalism ever, probably on a par with the obliteration of the Doric Portico at Euston. The fact that it was undertaken by a body supposedly devoted to the preservation of railway history can only add nausea to the whole proceedings.　　*Ken Fairey*

MANCHESTER

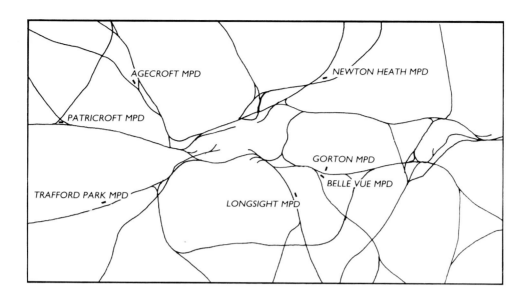

9A LONGSIGHT

Location: East of the Stockport Edgeley line, south of Manchester Piccadilly Station. (OS Map Ref: SJ867963)

Directions: Turn left outside of the main entrance to the station into London Road, continue into Downing Street and Ardwick Green South and fork left into Hyde Road. After about 1 mile, fork right into Redgate Lane and a cinder path leads to the shed from the right hand side.

Closed: February 14th, 1965 (Steam)

Description: A large shed complex consisting of 2 brick built through road buildings, the 8TS North Shed and the 12TS South Shed. The latter was converted into a 6TS Diesel Depot in 1957.

Post Closure History: *Still standing. In use as carriage and diesel depot (Codes MA and LO). (1990)*

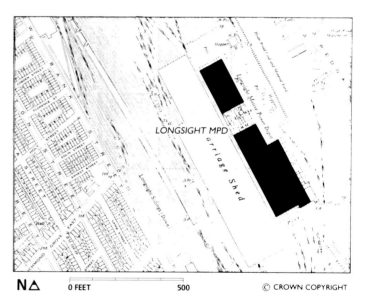

Map Dated: 1951

Site Location: East of the city centre, on the south side of Hyde Road (A57)

Track Status: Line operational.

The 'South Shed', occupied by ex-LMS steam locomotives, at **LONGSIGHT MPD** on September 27th, 1959. Converted from a twelve to six track straighthouse in 1957, the new building was constructed with diesel traction in mind, and now forms part of Longsight Diesel Depot.
WT Stubbs Collection

10C PATRICROFT

Location: In the fork of the Eccles to Patricroft and Monton Green lines. (OS Map Ref: SJ768989)

Directions: From Patricroft Station: Turn left along a narrow road running parallel to the railway line, continue into Hampden Grove and a footbridge on the left hand side leads to the shed.

Closed: July 1st, 1968.

Description: An unusual arrangement of brick built 8TS and 10TS sheds in an 'L' shape.

Post Closure History: Demolished.

The large **PATRICROFT MPD** viewed from the footbridge on August 22nd, 1959. The 8TS shed is to the left of the picture, with the 10TS building running at right angles and visible behind the coaling tower.
Ken Fairey

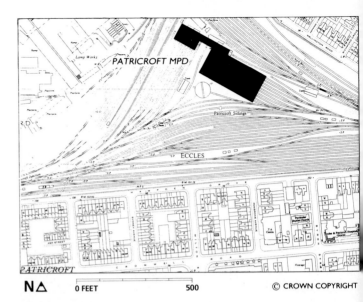

N△ 　 0 FEET 　 500 　 © CROWN COPYRIGHT

Map Dated: 1951

Site Location: West of the city centre, on the north side of Liverpool Road (A57)

Track Status: Patricroft Station and Patricroft to Eccles line are operational. All other lines lifted.

13A TRAFFORD PARK

Location: North of the line, about 1 mile east of Trafford Park & Stretford Station. (OS Map Ref: SJ804963)

Directions: Turn right outside of the west exit of Warwick Road Station, along Warwick Road, continue into Warwick Road North and turn left into Railway Road. A cinder path on the right hand side (opposite the end of Ravenswood Road) leads to the shed.

Closed: March 4th, 1968.

Description: A very dilapidated brick built 20TS dead ended shed.

Post Closure History: Demolished. Site of Freightliner depot. (1990)

The rambling and semi-derelict **TRAFFORD PARK MPD** on September 27th, 1959. Much of the roofing had disappeared by BR days and replacement was on a very modest scale, no attempt being made to restore it to its former covered accommodation.
WT Stubbs Collection

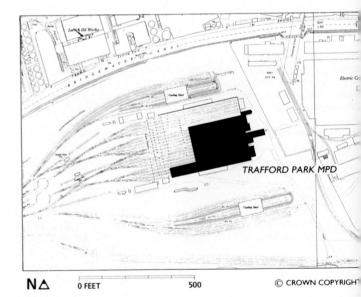

N△ 　 0 FEET 　 500 　 © CROWN COPYRIGHT

Map Dated: 1955

Site Location: South west of the city centre, on the north side of Chester Road (A56)

Track Status: Trafford Park Station and line are operational.

39A GORTON

Location: On the north side of the line between Ashburys and Gorton & Openshaw Stations. (OS Map Ref: SJ883973)

Directions: Turn left outside of Ashburys Station into Pottery Lane, turn right into Ashton Old Road and right into Widnes Street. The shed entrance is a door on the right hand side.

Closed: June 14th, 1965

Description: A brick built 18TS dead ended shed.

Post Closure History: *Demolished. Smithfield Market was opened on the site in 1975.*

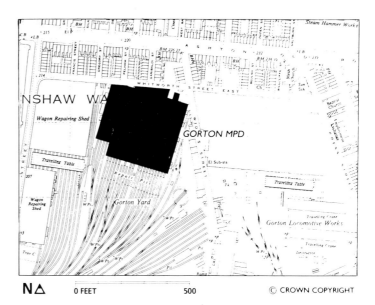

Map Dated: 1951
Site Location: East of the town centre, on the south side of Ashton Old Road (A635)
Track Status: Line operational.

A few locomotives are scattered around at a very empty **GORTON MPD** on a foggy October 15th, 1961.
WT Stubbs Collection

3B BELLE VUE

Location: In the fork of the Ashburys to Belle Vue (LMS) and Ashburys to Gorton (LNER) Lines. (OS Map Ref: SJ880970)

Directions: Turn right outside of Belle Vue Station into Station Road and at the end of this road turn right into Church Lane. Turn left into Taylor Street, left into Gorton Lane and right into Preston Street. A path leads to the shed from the left hand side, just before the bridge.

Closed: April 16th, 1956.

Description: A brick built roundhouse.

Post Closure History: *Still Standing. In use by scrap dealers. (1990)*

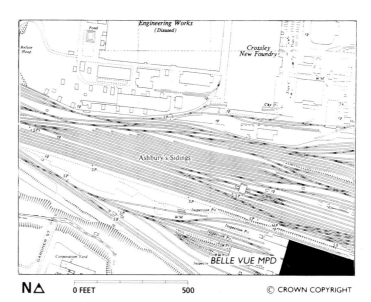

Map Dated: 1951
Site Location: East of the city centre, on the south side of Old Ashton Road (A635)
Track Status: Belle Vue Station and lines are operational.

A solitary ex-LMS Class 4F 0-6-0 locomotive stands outside of **BELLE VUE MPD** on April 18th, 1954.
Bernard Matthews Collection

26A NEWTON HEATH

Location: In the fork of the Miles Platting to Dean Lane and Newton Heath lines. (OS Map Ref: SD877009)

Directions: A broad path, on the west side of Dean Lane and between Dean Lane and Newton Heath Stations, leads to the shed.

Closed: July 1st, 1968.

Description: A brick built 23TS through road shed.

Post Closure History: *Most of the buildings were demolished to make way for a small Diesel Depot (Code NH) (1988).*

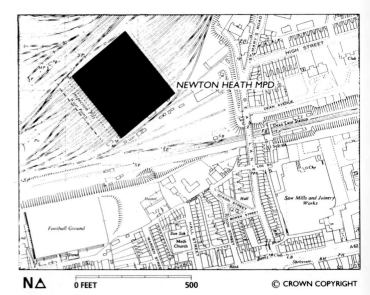

A section of the southern end of the huge **NEWTON HEATH MPD** on August 8th, 1958.
Alec Swain

Map Dated: 1951

Site Location: North east of city centre, on the north side of Oldham Road (A62)

Track Status: Lines operational.

26B AGECROFT

Location: In the fork of the Pendleton Broad Street to Swinton and Pendleton Broad Street to Clifton Junction lines. (OS Map Ref: SD805007)

Directions: Turn right outside Pendleton Broad Street Station into Broughton Road. Turn left into Whit Lane and continue into Langley Road, turning left into Tagge Lane. Cross the line and a path leads from the left hand side to the shed.

Closed: October 17th, 1966.

Description: A brick built 8TS dead ended shed, latterly in a very dilapidated condition with part of the roof missing.

Post Closure History: *Demolished shortly after closure.*

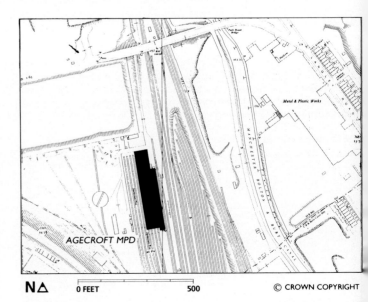

AGECROFT MPD on April 10th, 1966.
WT Stubbs

Map Dated: 1954

Site Location: North west of the city centre, on the north side of Bolton Road (A6)

Track Status: Pendleton Station and the Swinton line are operational.

LIVERPOOL

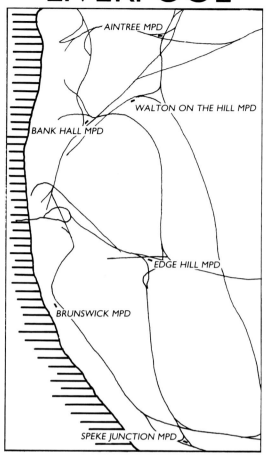

8A EDGE HILL

Location: Amongst a maze of lines,east of the junction of the Edge Hill to Mossley and Broad Green lines. (OS Map Ref: SJ384901)

Directions: Turn right outside the station along Tunnel Road, right into Wavertree Road and proceed into Picton Road. Turn left into Tiverton Street, just past the railway bridge, and a cinder path leads through a tunnel from the end of this road, to the shed.

Closed: May 6th, 1968

Description: A brick built 19TS shed with 6 through roads. A 6 track section of the dead ended portion was demolished and replaced by a small 2TS diesel depot.

Post Closure History: The remainder of the steam shed was demolished, leaving the diesel depot (Code EG). This has since been closed and was itself demolished on September 26th, 1986.

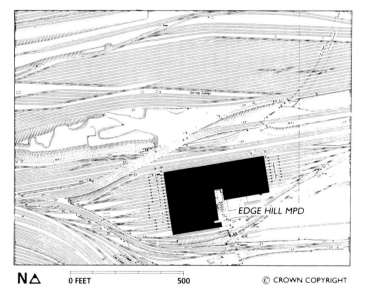

Map Dated: 1952

Site Location: East of the city centre, on the south side of Edge Lane (A5047)

Track Status: Line operational.

All the ex-LMS pacifics had gone by the time this view of **EDGE HILL MPD** was taken on October 28th, 1966, with the exception of a couple of 'Jinties' the yard being dominated by Stanier designs.
Allan Sommerfield Collection

8C SPEKE JUNCTION

Location: In the triangle of the Allerton to Garston Docks to Ditton Junction lines. (OS Map Ref: SJ414844)
Directions: Turn left outside of Allerton Station along Woolton Road, turn left into Horrocks Avenue, left into Speke Road, cross the railway bridge and turn left into Vineyard Street. Proceed under the bridge and a cinder path, on the right hand side leads to the shed.
Closed: May 6th, 1968.
Description: A brick built 12TS dead ended shed.
Post Closure History: Demolished. Site occupied by sidings. (1989)

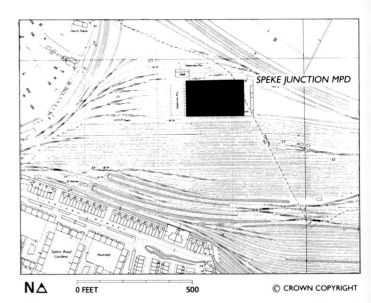

© CROWN COPYRIGHT

A general view of **SPEKE JUNCTION MPD** on April 10th, 1966.   *WT Stubbs*

Map Dated: 1953
Site Location: South of the city centre, on the north side of Speke Road (A561)
Track Status: Lines operational.

13E BRUNSWICK

Location: On the north side of the line, east of Liverpool Central Station. (OS Map Ref: SJ353876)
Directions: Turn left outside Liverpool Central Station into Ranelagh Street, left into Bold Street and right into Slater Street. Turn left at the end into Duke Street, first right into Kent Street and bear left at the end into Jamaica Street. Continue into Grafton Street and a gate on the right hand side leads to the shed via a flight of steps.
Closed: September 12th, 1961.
Description: A very cramped brick built 5TS dead ended shed.
Post Closure History: Demolished. The outer wall of the shed is still standing and forms part of the boundary of a site holding a Gasometer. Site unused. (1990)

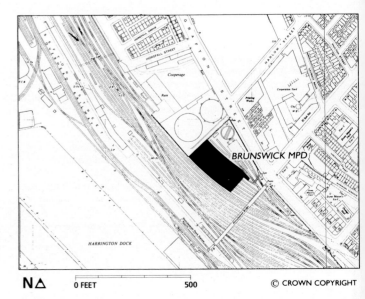

© CROWN COPYRIGHT

Map Dated: 1954
Site Location: South of the city centre, on the east side of Harrington Dock.
Track Status: Line operational.

An elevated view of **BRUNSWICK MPD** in 1953. This extremely cramped and awkwardly sited ex-CLC depot always seemed to be bursting at the seams with a cosmopolitan collection of ageing ex-LNER and LMS locomotives.
Chris Bush Collection

13F WALTON ON THE HILL

Location: East of the line, at the north end of Walton on the Hill Station. (OS Map Ref: SJ360951)
Directions: Entrance to the shed is effected from the station platform.
Closed: December 15th, 1963
Description: Originally a brick built 6TS dead ended shed, it was rebuilt as a 4TS structure in 1952.
Post Closure History: *Demolished. Site of Housing Estate. (1990)*

The abandoned and derelict **WALTON ON THE HILL MPD** on August 17th, 1971. *Allan Sommerfield Collection*

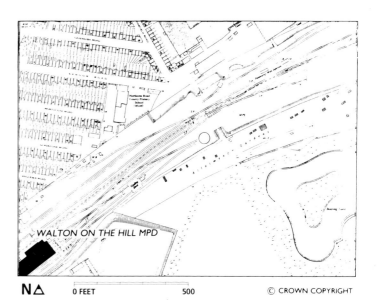

Map Dated: 1956
Site Location: North east of the city centre, on the east side of Rice Lane (A59)
Track Status: Walton on the Hill Station closed in 1918. Line lifted.

27A BANK HALL

Location: On the west side of the line between Sandhills and Kirkdale Stations. (OS Map Ref: SJ346939)
Directions: The shed entrance is on the opposite side of Stanley Road to Bank Hall Station.
Closed: October 17th, 1966.
Description: A brick built 8TS dead ended shed and a brick built 4TS through road shed.
Post Closure History: *Demolished, the site is now occupied by Kirkdale EMU depot. (1990)*

BR Standard Class 4 No. 75049 simmers outside of the four road shed at **BANK HALL MPD** on July 27th, 1966. *WT Stubbs*

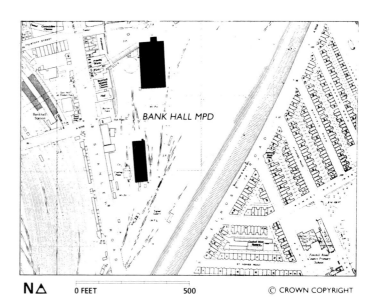

Map Dated: 1954
Site Location: North of the city centre, adjacent to the east side of Stanley Road (A567)
Track Status: Bank Hall Station and lines are operational.

27B AINTREE

Location: In the fork of the Ford to Aintree and Ford to Kirkby Goods lines. (OS Map Ref: SJ363975)

Directions: Turn left outside Aintree Sefton Arms Station into Park Lane. Turn right into Ormskirk Road and continue into Warbeck Moor. Pass under the railway bridge and turn second right into Helsby Road. Continue along a cinder path over one railway bridge, and under another. This path leads to the shed.

Closed: June 12th, 1967.

Description: A brick built 8TS dead ended shed.

Post Closure History: Still standing, with all track removed and in a vandalised state. (1990)

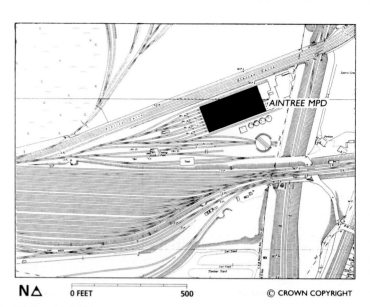

N△   0 FEET   500   © CROWN COPYRIGHT

Map Dated: 1958

Site Location: North of the city centre, on the west side of Warbeck Moor (A59)

Track Status: Aintree Station and lines operational.

AINTREE MPD on July 2nd, 1961.   *WT Stubbs Collection*

ENGINE SHED SOCIETY

For those interested in depots, the Engine Shed Society was formed in 1986 to bring together railway enthusiasts of a like mind. Through its quarterly magazine, LINK, members are kept up to date on shed developments and in-depth articles on shed related subjects feature in each issue. If sheds are your special interest then this society, with its nominal membership fee, may well be of interest. Please contact the Membership Secretary: D.Perkin, 59 Fulmar Drive, SALE, Cheshire M33 4WH for full details and application form.

STOKE MPD (Ken Fairey)

PART TWELVE

YORKSHIRE

YORKSHIRE

YORKSHIRE

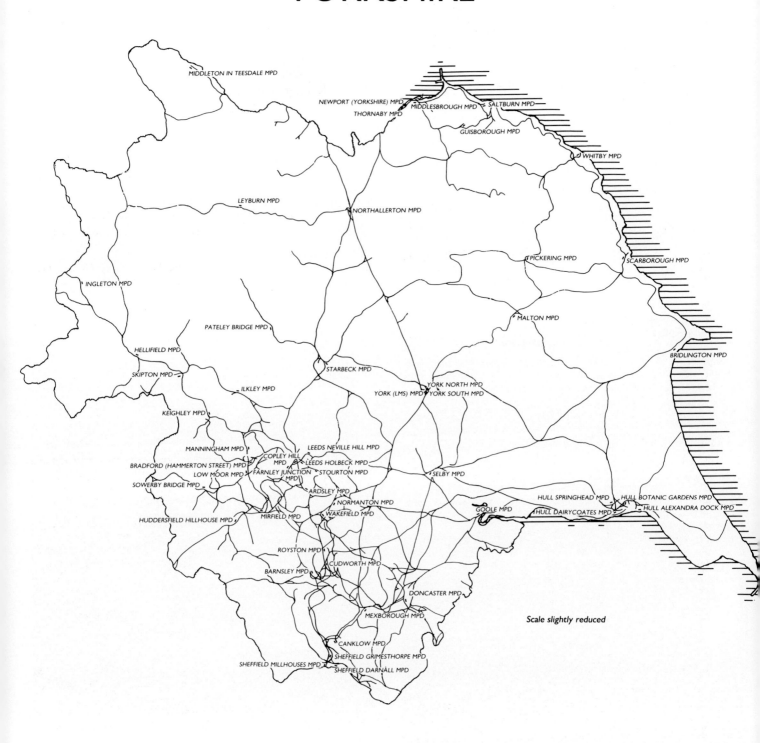

MIDDLETON IN TEESDALE MPD

NEWPORT (YORKSHIRE) MPD — MIDDLESBROUGH MPD — SALTBURN MPD
THORNABY MPD

GUISBOROUGH MPD

WHITBY MPD

LEYBURN MPD

NORTHALLERTON MPD

PICKERING MPD   SCARBOROUGH MPD

INGLETON MPD

MALTON MPD

PATELEY BRIDGE MPD

HELLIFIELD MPD

BRIDLINGTON MPD

SKIPTON MPD

STARBECK MPD

ILKLEY MPD

YORK NORTH MPD
YORK (LMS) MPD — YORK SOUTH MPD

KEIGHLEY MPD

LEEDS NEVILLE HILL MPD
MANNINGHAM MPD   COPLEY HILL MPD — LEEDS HOLBECK MPD
BRADFORD (HAMMERTON STREET) MPD   FARNLEY JUNCTION MPD — STOURTON MPD
LOW MOOR MPD   MPD
SOWERBY BRIDGE MPD   ARDSLEY MPD   SELBY MPD
                              HULL SPRINGHEAD MPD — HULL BOTANIC GARDENS MPD
NORMANTON MPD
GOOLE MPD — HULL DAIRYCOATES MPD — HULL ALEXANDRA DOCK MPD
HUDDERSFIELD HILLHOUSE MPD   MIRFIELD MPD   WAKEFIELD MPD

ROYSTON MPD

CUDWORTH MPD

BARNSLEY MPD

DONCASTER MPD

MEXBOROUGH MPD   *Scale slightly reduced*

CANKLOW MPD
SHEFFIELD GRIMESTHORPE MPD
SHEFFIELD MILLHOUSES MPD
SHEFFIELD DARNALL MPD

36A DONCASTER

Location: On the east side of the line, south of Doncaster Station. (OS Map Ref: SE576017)

Directions: Cross the station yard, turn right into Station Road, right into St. Sepulchre Gate and continue for some distance before turning left into St. Swithin Terrace, just before the railway bridge. Proceed along Kellam Street to the end, turn right into Oak Terrace and the shed entrance is at the end of this road.

Closed: April 1966 (Steam)

Description: A brick built 11TS through road shed.

Post Closure History: *Still standing. In use as a diesel depot (Code DR) (1990)*

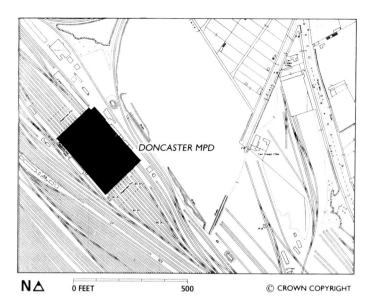

DONCASTER MPD with A3 and A1 Class locomotives in the shed yard on May 26th, 1963. By this time the ex-LNER pacifics had been relegated to semi-fast passenger and freight work.
Ken Fairey

Map Dated: 1961

Site Location: South of the town centre, on the west side of Decoy Bank.

Track Status: Doncaster Station and lines are operational.

36B MEXBOROUGH

Location: South of the line, west of Mexborough Station.(OS Map Ref: SK470995)

Directions: Turn right outside of the station along a cinder path, right under the bridge and right again along a path running parallel to the railway. This leads to the shed.

Closed: February 1964.

Description: A brick built 15TS dead ended shed.

Post Closure History: *Demolished. Site unused (1990)*

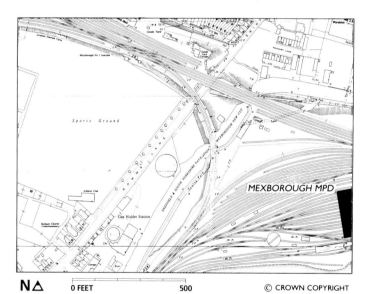

The large freight engine shed at **MEXBOROUGH MPD** on March 26th, 1961. Devoid of major mechanical aids for virtually the whole of its existence, BR finally got around to supplying a mechanical coaling plant in the early sixties! Rumour has it that the demolition contract was awarded whilst building was in progress. Perhaps not quite true but it was, nonetheless, an appalling waste of money and resources not entirely unique in those days of transition from steam to diesel.
WT Stubbs Collection

Map Dated: 1958

Site Location: South of the town centre, on the south side of Wath Road (A6023)

Track Status: Mexborough Station and line are operational.

19A SHEFFIELD GRIMESTHORPE

Location: East of the line, south of Brightside Station. (OS Map Ref: SK385907)

Directions: Turn left outside of Brightside Station into Station Lane, turn right into Meadowhall Road and proceed along Brightside Lane. The shed entrance is on the right hand side immediately before Newhall Road.

Closed: September 11th, 1961

Description: A brick built roundhouse shed.

Post Closure History: *Demolished. Site now occupied by sidings. (1990)*

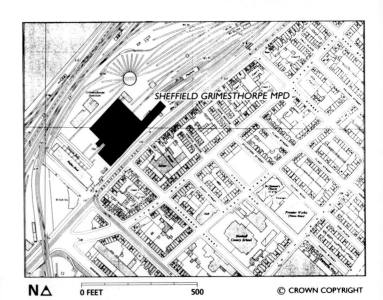

N△   0 FEET   500   © CROWN COPYRIGHT

Map Dated: 1955
Site Location: North east of city centre, adjacent to the north side of Brightside Lane (A6109)
Track Status: Brightside Station and line are operational.

Two Class 46 Diesel Locomotives stable outside of the closed **SHEFFIELD GRIMESTHORPE MPD** on October 13th, 1963.   *WT Stubbs Collection*

19B MILLHOUSES

Location: West of the line, north of Millhouses & Ecclesall Station. (OS Map Ref: SK340837)

Directions: A cinder path runs northwards along the side of the line from Millhouses & Ecclesall Station to the shed.

Closed: January 1st, 1962.

Description: A brick built 8TS dead ended shed.

Post Closure History: *Still Standing. In industrial use. (1990)*

MILLHOUSES MPD in March 1954.   *Photomatic*

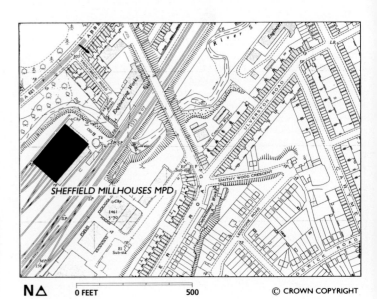

N△   0 FEET   500   © CROWN COPYRIGHT

Map Dated: 1952
Site Location: South west of city centre, on the east side of Abbeydale Road (A621)
Track Status: Millhouses & Ecclesall Station closed in 1968. Line operational. Station earmarked for re-opening by South Yorkshire PTE.

39B SHEFFIELD (DARNALL)

Location: South of the line, west of Darnall Station. (OS Map Ref: SK386877)

Directions: Turn into Station Road, outside of the station, turn left into Main Road, bear left into Staniforth Road, turn left into Ribston Road and proceed along Bridge Road. A Private Road leads to the shed from the left hand side just past the railway bridge.

Closed: June 17th, 1963 (Steam). October 4th 1965 (Totally)

Description: A brick built 10TS through road shed.

Post Closure History: *Still Standing. Roof missing and disused. (1989)*

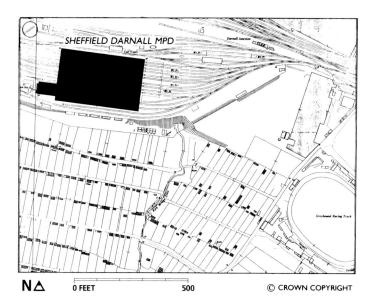

NΔ   0 FEET   500   © CROWN COPYRIGHT

Map Dated: 1955

Site Location: East of the city centre, on the south side of Staniforth Road (B6200)

Track Status: Darnall Station and line are operational.

The roofless former depot at **DARNALL MPD** on April 16th, 1989. Although the depot was empty of rolling stock some of the tracks were still shiny.

Brian Cuttell

19C CANKLOW

Location: On the west side of the Rotherham Masborough to Staveley line about 2 miles south of Masborough. (OS Map Ref: SK426898)

Directions: Go straight ahead out of Masborough Station along Station Road and proceed along Masborough Street and Main Street. Turn right at the end into Westgate, continue into Canklow Road and after about a mile and a quarter turn right into Bawtry Road. Proceed under the railway bridge and turn immediate left into White Hill Lane. The shed entrance is on the left hand side about 300 yards along.

Closed: October 11th, 1965:

Description: A brick built roundhouse.

Post Closure History: *Demolished. Now site of a Housing Estate (1990).*

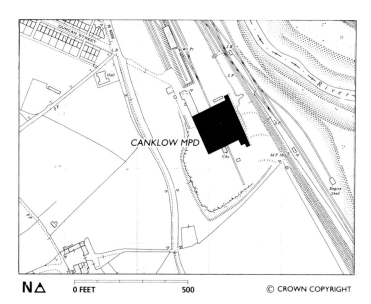

NΔ   0 FEET   500   © CROWN COPYRIGHT

Map Dated: 1956

Site Location: South of the town centre, on the west side of West Bawtry Road (A631)

Track Status: Line operational. Masborough Station closed.

A general view of the yard and buildings at **CANKLOW MPD** taken in the mid-sixties, just before closure.   *Bernard Matthews Collection*

20A LEEDS HOLBECK

Location: West of the Woodlesford line, about half a mile south of Leeds City Station. (OS Map Ref: SE292325)

Directions: Turn sharp right outside of the station into Bishopsgate, right into Neville Street, proceed along Victoria Road and turn right into Manor Road. Turn left at the end into Marshall Street, right into Nineveh Road and the shed entrance is on the right hand side.

Closed: October 2nd, 1967 (Steam).

Description: Consisting of two brick built roundhouses.

Post Closure History: The buildings were demolished in 1970 and a small diesel depot (code HO) erected. Still operational in 1990.

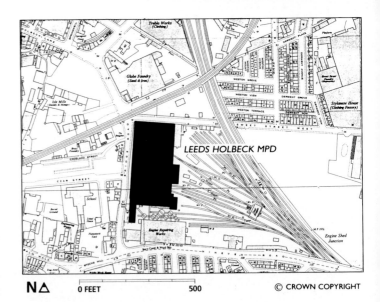

Map Dated: 1954
Site Location: South of the city centre, on the east side of the A643
Track Status: Line operational

Part of **LEEDS HOLBECK MPD**, the old Erecting Shop on the west side of the site, had been taken over to service Class 46 and other diesel types by September 15th, 1963 as this view shows. The roundhouse portion, on the right of the picture, accommodated the steam locomotives until closure.   *WT Stubbs Collection*

20B STOURTON

Location: West of the line, about 3 miles north of Woodlesford Station. (OS Map Ref: SE323303)

Directions: From Leeds Central Station: Turn right into Wellington Street, proceed into City Square, turn right into Bishopsgate, continue into Swinegate and turn right into Bridge End. Proceed along Hunslet Road and Low Road, fork right into Wakefield Road, cross the railway bridge and a cinder path, on the left hand side, leads to the shed.

Closed: January 1967.

Description: A brick built roundhouse.

Post Closure History: Demolished. Site now occupied by roadway and commercial development. (1990)

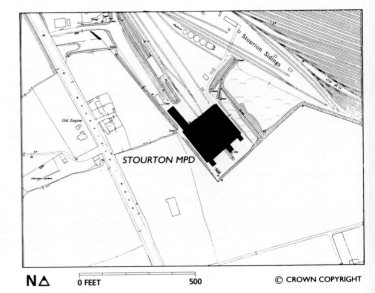

Map Dated: 1953
Site Location: South east of city centre, on the east side of M1 Junction 43.
Track Status: Line operational.

A general view of the coaling stage and yard at **STOURTON MPD** on September 17th, 1961.
WT Stubbs Collection

37B LEEDS COPLEY HILL

Location: In the triangle formed by the Leeds Central, Armley Moor and Ardsley lines. (OS Map Ref: SE281326)

Directions: Turn left outside of Leeds City Station into City Square, left again into Aire Street and proceed along Whitehall Road. Turn right into Copley Hill and the shed entrance is a door in the wall on the left hand side, just past the first bridge.

Closed: September 7th, 1964.

Description: A brick built 5TS through road shed.

Post Closure History: Demolished. The whole site is an industrial estate. (1990)

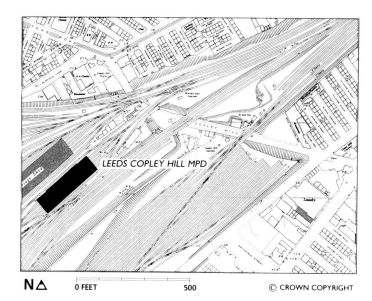

Map Dated: 1954
Site Location: West of the city centre, on the north side of Whitehall Road (A58)
Track Status: Lines operational.

A quiet interlude at **LEEDS COPLEY HILL MPD** on September 15th, 1963.
WT Stubbs Collection

37A ARDSLEY

Location: On the east side of the line, south of Ardsley Station. (OS Map Ref: SE312259)

Directions: A cinder path leads from the east side of Stanhope Road to the shed, from a point opposite the eastern end of the station.

Closed: October 1965

Description: A brick built 8TS through road shed

Post Closure History: Demolished.

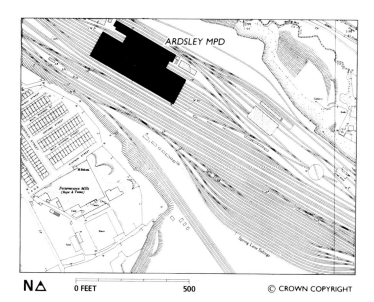

Map Dated: 1953
Site Location: South of Leeds, north of the A650
Track Status: Ardsley Station closed in 1964. Line operational.

ARDSLEY MPD on April 28th, 1957.   *Ken Fairey*

25G FARNLEY JUNCTION

Location: On the west side of the line from Leeds to Morley Low, south of Farnley & Wortley Station. (OS Map Ref: SE271312)
Directions: From Leeds City Station: Turn left outside the station into City Square, left into Aire Street and continue into Whitehall Road. After about 1.75 miles turn right into Royds Lane and bear right along a rough road, just before a railway bridge, leading up a hill. A cinder path leads to the shed at the top of this hill.
Closed: November 1966
Description: A brick built 12TS dead ended shed.
Post Closure History: *Demolished. Site unused (1987)*

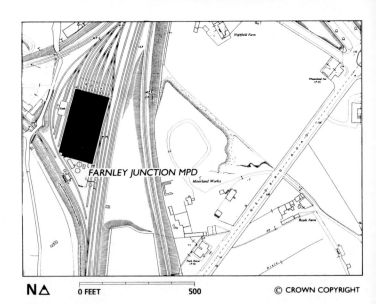

N△   0 FEET   500   © CROWN COPYRIGHT

Map Dated: 1955
Site Location: South west of the city centre, on the west side of Gelderd Road (A62).
Track Status: Line operational.

FARNLEY JUNCTION MPD in BR days.   *Bernard Matthews Collection*

50B LEEDS NEVILLE HILL

Location: North of the Cross Gates line, about 2 miles east of Leeds City Station. (OS Map Ref: SE330331)
Directions: Turn right outside of Leeds Central Station into Wellington Street, proceed through City Square and along Boar Lane and Duncan Street. Turn left into Call Lane, right into New York Street, continue along York Lane and turn right into York Road. After about 1.25 miles turn right into Osmondthorpe Lane and the shed entrance is on the right hand side.
Closed: June 12th, 1966 (Steam).
Description: A brick built four roundhouse shed.
Post Closure History: *Still standing. In use as a Diesel Depot (Code NL).*

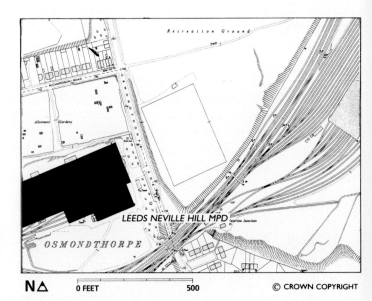

N△   0 FEET   500   © CROWN COPYRIGHT

Map Dated: 1952
Site Location: East of the city centre, on the south side of York Road (A64).
Track Status: Line operational.
The shed was rebuilt in 1960 to incorporate just 2 turntables and stalls, the remainder converted for diesel use. Following closure to steam the whole building was adapted as a straighthouse.

LEEDS NEVILLE HILL MPD on September 15th, 1963. Destined to be the main Diesel depot for the area, steam and diesel locomotives co-existed uneasily for a few years after the shed rebuilding started in 1960, until the diesels took over completely in 1966. The two remaining turntables were removed and the whole building became one large straighthouse.   *WT Stubbs Collection*

20C ROYSTON

Location: East of the line, south of Royston & Notton Station. (OS Map Ref: SE375113)

Directions: A pathway leads to the shed from the end of Platform 4.

Closed: November 6th, 1967.

Description: A brick built 10TS dead ended shed.

Post Closure History: Demolished. Site unused. (1980)

ROYSTON MPD on September 29th, 1963.   *WT Stubbs Collection*

On a visit to the depot on May 28th, 1967, less than three months before closure, there were a total of 26 locomotives, incredibly every one was an ex-LMS Stanier Class 8F 2–8–0. The number of occasions that a shed held only one class of locomotive in those sort of numbers must be very few.

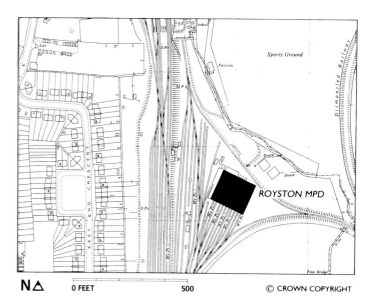

N △   0 FEET   500   © CROWN COPYRIGHT

Map Dated: 1962

Site Location: On the east side of Royston, south of Midland Road (B6428)

Track Status: Royston & Notton Station closed in 1968. Line operational.

20D NORMANTON

Location: East of the line, north of Normanton Station. (OS Map Ref: SE384232)

Directions: Go straight ahead out of the station along the approach road, turn left into Station Lane and proceed along a path running parallel to the tracks. The shed entrance is a gate in Altofts Lane at the end of this pathway.

Closed: January 1st, 1968.

Description: A brick built 5TS dead ended shed.

Post Closure History: Demolished. Site unused. (1976)

The straighthouse at **NORMANTON MPD** on September 17th, 1961.
WT Stubbs Collection

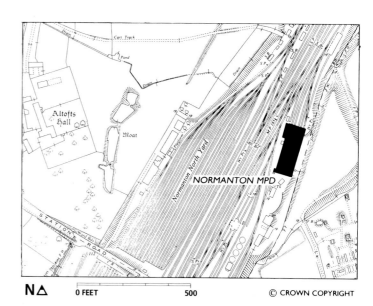

N △   0 FEET   500   © CROWN COPYRIGHT

Map Dated: 1955

Site Location: West of the town centre, on the west side of the A655.

Track Status: Normanton Station and line are operational.

20E MANNINGHAM

Location: On the east side of Bradford Manningham Station. (OS Map Ref: SE158350)

Directions: A path leads from the north end of the southbound platform to the shed.

Closed: April 30th, 1967.

Description: A brick built Roundhouse.

Post Closure History: Demolished. Site of industrial development. (1990)

A general view of the ex-MR roundhouse at **MANNINGHAM MPD** on September 10th, 1961.
WT Stubbs

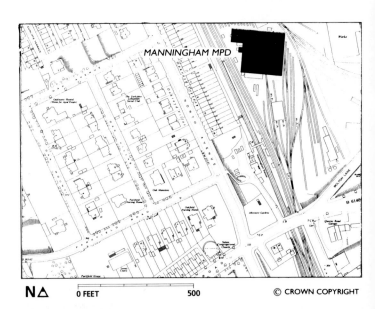

N△ 0 FEET 500 © CROWN COPYRIGHT

Map Dated: 1959

Site Location: North of the town centre, on the north side of Queen's Road (A650)

Track Status: Manningham Station closed in 1965. Line operational.

37C BRADFORD (HAMMERTON STREET)

Location: On the south side of the Laisterdyke line, about 1200 yards from Bradford Exchange Station. (OS Map Ref: SE174324)

Directions: Leave the station by the approach road, turn left into Bridge Street, continue into Wakefield Road and then fork left into Bowling Back Lane. The shed entrance is on the left hand side.

Closed: January 1958 (Steam)

Description: A brick built 11TS dead ended shed.

Post Closure History: Used as a diesel and DMU depot (Code HS) until 1987. Still Standing in a derelict condition.

BRADFORD (HAMMERTON STREET) MPD had succumbed to total dieselisation when viewed on September 10th, 1961.
WT Stubbs

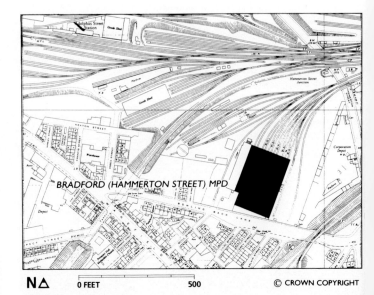

N△ 0 FEET 500 © CROWN COPYRIGHT

Map Dated: 1958

Site Location: East of the town centre, on the north side of Wakefield Road (A650)

Track Status: Bradford Exchange Station is closed, having been replaced by the new Bradford Interchange Station

The Diesel Depot officially closed on May 13th, 1984

23A SKIPTON

Location: South of the line, west of Skipton Station.(OS Map Ref: SD978512)

Directions: Turn left outside of the station, proceed up Carleton New Road, on the right hand side of the main road, and turn left over the bridge. Turn right at the end into a lane running parallel to the track and the shed entrance is on the left hand side.

Closed: April 3rd, 1967

Description: Composed of two adjoining 3TS dead ended sheds, originally of wooden construction but rebuilt by BR in brick.

Post Closure History: Still Standing. In use as a local authority depot. (1989)

The shed buildings at **SKIPTON MPD** on June 17th, 1962. Formerly of wood, they were rebuilt in brick by BR in the early 1950s. *WT Stubbs Collection*

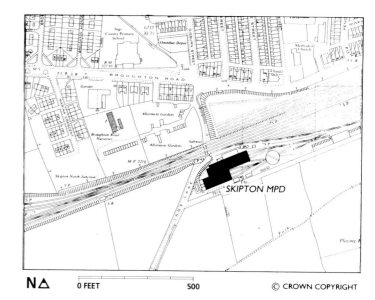

N△ 0 FEET 500 © CROWN COPYRIGHT

Map Dated: 1965
Site Location: West of town centre, on the south side of Broughton Road.
Track Status: Skipton Station and line are operational.

20F(s) KEIGHLEY

Location: East of the line, north of Keighley Station. (OS Map Ref: SE063416)

Directions: Turn left outside of the station along Bradford Road, first right along Cavendish Street and right into Lawkholme Lane. Cross the railway bridge and the shed entrance is on the left hand side.

Closed: June 18th, 1962

Description: A brick built 4TS dead ended shed.

Post Closure History: Demolished.

KEIGHLEY MPD at the point of closure on June 17th, 1962. This view shows how the covered accommodation had been reduced to two roads only in the last years of operation. *WT Stubbs Collection*

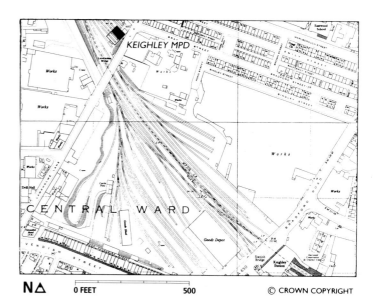

N△ 0 FEET 500 © CROWN COPYRIGHT

Map Dated: 1969
Site Location: North of town centre.
Track Status: Keighley Station and line operational.

23B HELLIFIELD

Location: North of the line, at the west end of Hellifield Station. (OS Map Ref: SD850574)

Directions: A boarded crossing runs from the station platforms to the shed.

Closed: June 17th, 1963.

Description: A brick built 4TS through road shed.

Post Closure History: *Upon closure the shed was renovated and used for the storage of preserved locomotives pending the opening of York Museum. Now demolished. Site unused. (1990)*

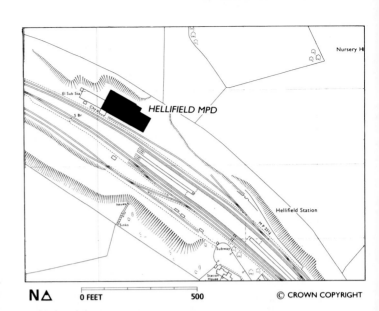

HELLIFIELD MPD on June 1st, 1963, a few days before closure.
WT Stubbs Collection

Map Dated: 1974

Site Location: North of the town centre, on the north side of the A65.

Track Status: Hellifield Station and line are operational.

23B(s) INGLETON

Location: East of the line, south of Ingleton Station. (OS Map Ref: SD6977729)

Directions: Turn left outside of the station, left along Railway Terrace, pass under the railway bridge and turn right into the Goods Yard. The shed is in this yard.

Closed: January 30th, 1954.

Description: A wooden built 1TS dead ended shed.

Post Closure History: *Demolished.*

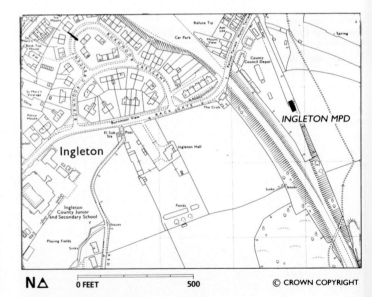

The semi-derelict wooden built **INGLETON MPD** in BR days.
Bernard Matthews Collection

Map Dated: 1972 (Shed Superimposed)

Site Location: East of the village centre

Track Status: Ingleton Station closed in 1954. Line lifted.

25A WAKEFIELD

Location: East of the Pontefract line, running south from the east end of Wakefield Kirkgate Station. (OS Map Ref: SE348195)

Directions: Turn left outside of the station into Station Passage, left into Kirkgate, cross the new bridge and fork left into Doncaster Road. Turn left into Elmtree Street and a footbridge leads to the shed from the end of this street.

Closed: June 3rd, 1967.

Description: A brick built 8TS through road shed.

Post Closure History: *Still Standing. Used as a wagon works following closure until 1988. Now abandoned. (1990)*

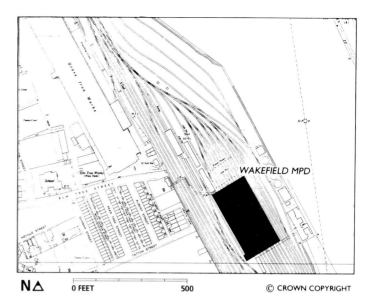

A thoroughly mixed bag of ex-WD and former LMS and LNER designs create a busy scene at **WAKEFIELD MPD** on September 17th, 1961.

WT Stubbs Collection

Map Dated: 1954

Site Location: South of the town centre, on the south bank of the River Calder.

Track Status: Wakefield Kirkgate Station and line are operational.

25B HUDDERSFIELD HILLHOUSE

Location: West of the line, north of Huddersfield Station. (OS Map Ref: SE149181)

Directions: Leave the station, cross St.Georges Square, turn left into John William Street, right into Viaduct Street and turn left into Bradford Road. Pass under the bridge, turn right into Alder Street and a path leads over a footbridge to the shed, from a gate on the right hand side.

Closed: January 2nd, 1967.

Description: A stone built 6TS shed with 4 through roads, adjoined by a smaller stone built 2TS extension.

Post Closure History: *Demolished.*

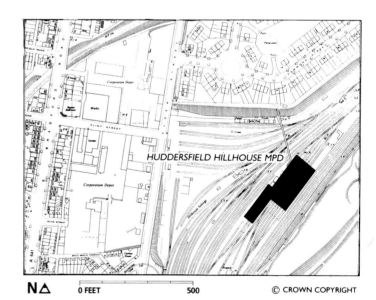

HUDDERSFIELD HILLHOUSE MPD on September 17th, 1961.

WT Stubbs Collection

Map Dated: 1960

Site Location: North of the town, on the east side of Bradford Road (A641)

Track Status: Huddersfield Station and line are operational.

25C GOOLE

Location: On the north side of the line, just west of Goole West Junction, and about 1.25 miles west of Goole Station. (OS Map Ref: SE726224)
Directions: Cross Booth Ferry Road outside of the station into Mariners Street, bear right past a large island in the middle of the road and enter a fenced footpath on the right hand side. Proceed along this path which eventually runs alongside the Docks Goods Line. Pass under the Doncaster line railway bridge and a boarded crossing leads to the shed.
Closed: May 8th, 1967.
Description: A 6TS brick built dead ended shed.
Post Closure History: Demolished. Site unused (1976)

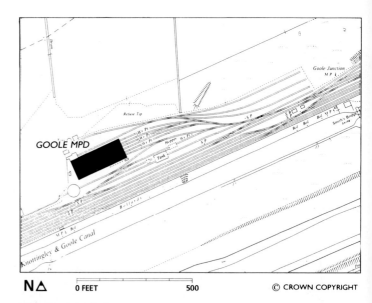

A large variety of locomotives, ranging from 2–8–0 WD Austerities to ex-L&Y 0–4–0STs in the shed yard at **GOOLE MPD** on July 24th, 1960.   Ken Fairey

Map Dated: 1965
Site Location: West of the town centre, north of Dutch River.
Track Status: Line operational.

25D MIRFIELD

Location: North of the line, west of Mirfield Station. (OS Map Ref: SE196199)
Directions: Turn left outside of the station along Back Station Road, left into Newgate, right into Chadwick Lane and turn right into Woodend Road. This road follows the railway line and leads to the shed.
Closed: April 1967.
Description: A brick built 8TS dead ended shed.
Post Closure History: Still Standing, although in a very dilapidated condition. Site owned by Pattersons Transport and many scrap vehicles litter the area. (1987)

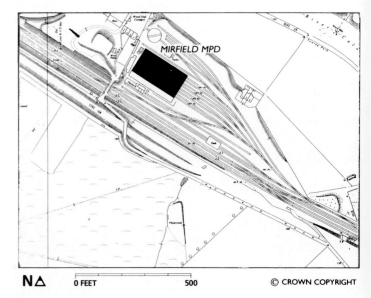

MIRFIELD MPD on September 17th, 1961.   *WT Stubbs Collection*

Map Dated: 1958
Site Location: West of the town centre, on the south side of Huddersfield Road (A544)
Track Status: Mirfield Station and line are operational.

25E SOWERBY BRIDGE

Location: North of the line, west of Sowerby Bridge Station. (OS Map Ref: SE055236)

Directions: Leave the station and proceed along Station Road, turn right into Town Hall, pass under the railway bridge and turn left into Walton Street. A gate, on the left hand side leads to the shed via a set of steps.

Closed: January 4th, 1964.

Description: A stone built 6TS dead ended shed.

Post Closure History: *Demolished. Site unused, although part of the shed yard has been developed for industrial use. (1982)*

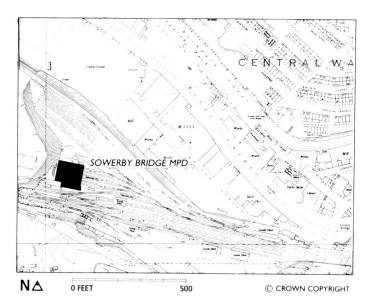

N△   0 FEET   500   © CROWN COPYRIGHT

Map Dated: 1964
Site Location: West of the town centre, on the west side of the A58
Track Status: Sowerby Bridge Station and line are operational.

SOWERBY BRIDGE MPD on September 10th, 1961.   *WT Stubbs*

25F LOW MOOR

Location: On the north side of Low Moor Station. (OS Map Ref: SE166284)

Directions: Turn right outside of the station into Cleckheaton Road and right again into Lockwood Street. Proceed along the cinder path and the shed entrance is on the right hand side.

Closed: October 2nd, 1967.

Description: A brick built 6TS dead ended shed.

Post Closure History: *Demolished.*

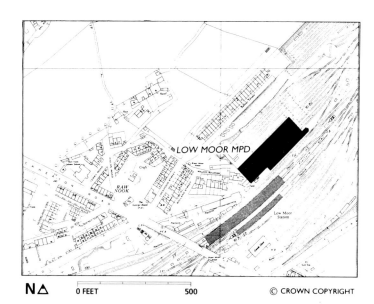

N△   0 FEET   500   © CROWN COPYRIGHT

Map Dated: 1957
Site Location: South of Bradford town centre, on the north side of Cleckheaton Road (A638)
Track Status: Low Moor Station closed in 1965. Line operational.

LOW MOOR MPD on September 15th, 1963.   *WT Stubbs Collection*

20E(s) ILKLEY

Location: On the north side of the line, at the east end of Ilkley Station. (OS Map Ref: SE123476)
Directions: Entrance to the shed is effected from the station platform.
Closed: January 5th, 1959.
Description: A brick built 2TS dead ended shed.
Post Closure History: Demolished. Site occupied by Industrial Premises.

The brick built **ILKLEY MPD** on November 17th, 1957.   *Brian Hilton*

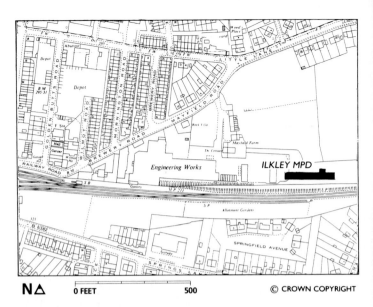

N△   0 FEET   500   © CROWN COPYRIGHT

Map Dated: 1969 (Shed Superimposed)
Site Location: East of the town centre, north of Springs Lane (B6382)
Track Status: Ilkley Station and line are operational.

50D(s) PATELEY BRIDGE

Location: West of the line, south of Pateley Bridge Station. (OS Map Ref: SE160653)
Directions: Entrance to the shed is effected from the station platform.
Closed: April 1st, 1951.
Description: A wooden built 1TS through road shed.
Post Closure History: Demolished. Site unused. (1975)

A pre-war view of the wooden built **PATELEY BRIDGE MPD**.
Allan Sommerfield Collection

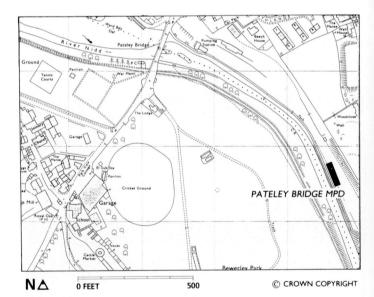

N△   0 FEET   500   © CROWN COPYRIGHT

Map Dated: 1975 (Shed Superimposed)
Site Location: South of the town centre, on the east bank of the River Nidd.
Track Status: Pateley Bridge Station closed in 1951. Line lifted.

50A YORK NORTH

Location: West of the main line, north of York Station. (OS Map Ref: SE520594)

Directions: Turn left outside of the station along Station Road, first left into Leeman Road, continue under the bridge and the shed entrance is on the right hand side.

Closed: June 1967 (Steam), March 1984 (Totally)

Description: Originally a brick built 4 roundhouse building, two of the roundhouses were converted into a 5TS dead ended shed in 1958.

Post Closure History: *The straighthouse portion became a Diesel Depot (Code YK) whilst the two roundhouses are now the National Railway Museum. It is planned to re-roof the museum building and remove one of the turntables. (1990)*

YORK NORTH MPD on August 21st, 1950.   *Brian Hilton*

50A(s) YORK (LMS)

Location: In a triangle of lines, west of the main line, at the south end of York Station. (OS Map Ref: SE593515)

Directions: A boarded crossing leads from the most westerly platforms of the station to York South shed. The shed is just beyond the South Shed complex.

Closed: 1948 *(Became part of York South Shed)*

Description: A brick built 3TS through road shed.

Post Closure History: *Stored locomotives for many years until closure of York South. Since demolished, the site is unused. (1990)*

Ex-LMS Class 4F 0–6–0 No. 44604 parked on one of the shed roads at **YORK (LMS) MPD** on August 21st, 1950. By this time the depot had lost its separate identity and was incorporated as part of York South MPD.   *Brian Hilton*

50A(s) YORK SOUTH

Location: In a triangle of lines, west of the main line at the south end of York Station. (OS Map Ref: SE593515)

Directions: A boarded crossing leads from the most westerly platforms of the station to the shed.

Closed: May 1961.

Description: A depot complex consisting of 2 brick built roundhouses. The former ex-LMS 3TS shed became part of the depot shortly after nationalisation.

Post Closure History: *Demolished. Site unused. (1990)*

Ex-LNER Class J25 0–6–0 No. 65698 in store outside one of the roundhouses at **YORK SOUTH MPD** on June 22nd, 1959.   *Ken Fairey*

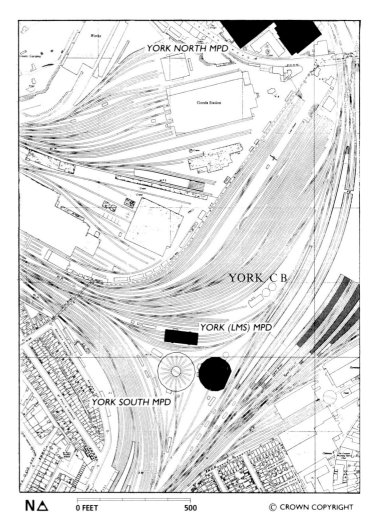

N△   0 FEET   500   © CROWN COPYRIGHT

Map Dated: 1962

Site Location: On the west side of the city.

Track Status: York Station and line are operational.

53A HULL DAIRYCOATES

Location: Amongst a maze of lines, south of the main line to Hessle and about 2.25 miles from Hull Station. (OS Map Ref: TA070260)

Directions: Turn right outside the station into Paragon Square, right into Carr Lane, left into Porter Street and bear right into Hessle Road. After about 1.25 miles turn left into Brighton Street and right into a Private Road. A footbridge leads to the shed from this road.

Closed: June 24th, 1967 (Steam), September 21st, 1970 (Totally).

Description: A massive shed site consisting of 6 brick built roundhouses and brick built 3TS and 2TS sheds.

Post Closure History: Part of the roundhouse used as a private road container depot, the crane shop used by the HLPG for a steam locomotive restoration centre, and the offices and some other buildings used by BR. (1988)

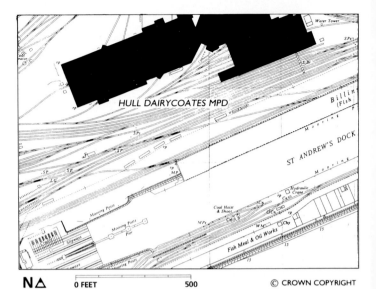

N△   0 FEET   500   © CROWN COPYRIGHT

Map Dated: 1951
Site Location: West of the town centre, on the south side of Hessle Road (A1105)
Track Status: Line operational.

Tank Engines cluster around one of the open air turntables and ex-LNER Class V2 2–6–2 locomotives stand outside of a portion of the huge shed at **HULL DAIRYCOATES MPD** on July 24th, 1960.
Ken Fairey

53B HULL BOTANIC GARDENS

Location: East of the line, south of Botanic Gardens Station. (OS Map Ref: TA081292)

Directions: Turn left outside of Hull Station into Paragon Square, proceed along Ferensway, bear left into Springbank, continuing for some distance and turn left into Derringham Street. Turn right into Kimberly Street and the shed entrance is at the end.

Closed: June 14th, 1959 (Steam).

Description: A brick built Double-Roundhouse shed.

Post Closure History: Still Standing. Converted to a straight shed and used for DMUs (Code BG) until 1987. Now in use as a fuelling point.

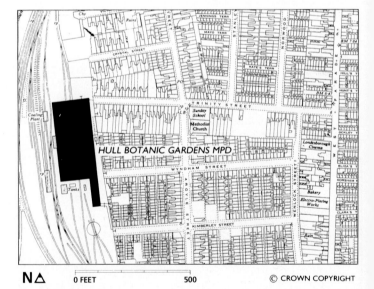

N△   0 FEET   500   © CROWN COPYRIGHT

Map Dated: 1950
Site Location: North of town centre, on the south side of Spring Bank.
Track Status: Botanic Gardens Station closed in 1964. Line operational.

The totally refurbished **HULL BOTANIC GARDENS MPD** plays host to a Class 03 Diesel Shunter and a couple of DMU sets on October 13th, 1963.
WT Stubbs Collection

53C HULL SPRINGHEAD

Location: North of the line, east of Springhead Halt. (OS Map Ref: TA051292)

Directions: Turn left outside of Hull Station into Paragon Square, proceed along Ferensway, bear left into Springbank and continue along Springbank West. A broad cinder path leads to the shed from the end of this road.

Closed: December 15th, 1958 (Steam), July 1961 (Totally).

Description: A brick built 8TS through road shed.

Post Closure History: Used for locomotive storage immediately after closure. Since demolished.

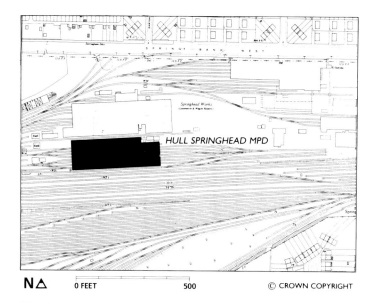

Map Dated: 1952
Site Location: North of the town centre, on the east side of the A1079.
Track Status: All lines lifted.

Goods Vans parked inside the remains of **HULL SPRINGHEAD MPD** on October 13th, 1963.
WT Stubbs Collection

53C(s) HULL ALEXANDRA DOCK

Location: In Hull Alexandra Docks.(OS Map Ref: TA127292)

Directions: Turn right outside of Hull Station into Paragon Square, left into Carr Lane, continue into Alfred Street and Gelder Street, crossing Drypool Bridge. Turn right into Great Union Street, bear left into Hedon Road and enter Alexandra Dock by the Main Gate. Bear left along the Dock Road and the shed is on the left hand side.

Closed: November 14th, 1960 (Steam), October 27th, 1963 (Totally).

Description: Consisting of 2 tracks and pits, with adjacent shed offices. There are no Shed Buildings.

Post Closure History: Lines lifted.

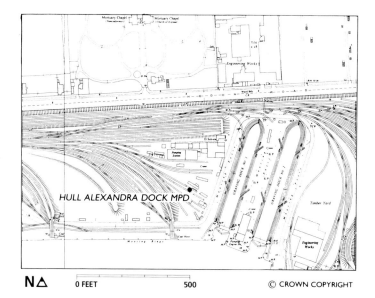

Map Dated: 1951
Site Location: East of town centre, on the south side of Hedon Road (A1033)
Track Status: Some lines lifted.

Steam and Diesel locomotives rub shoulders at **HULL ALEXANDRA DOCK MPD** on July 24th, 1960, a few months before the ex-LNER Tank Engines were finally ousted and the Class 08 Diesel Shunters took over all the duties. *Ken Fairey*

50C SELBY

Location: In the fork of the Selby to Leeds and East Coast Main Lines, south of Selby Station. (OS Map Ref: SE616319)
Directions: Turn left outside of the station along the approach road, climb the steps on to the road bridge and the shed entrance is on the opposite of the bridge some half way along.
Closed: September 13th, 1959.
Description: A brick built double-roundhouse shed.
Post Closure History: Demolished. Site unused. (1976)

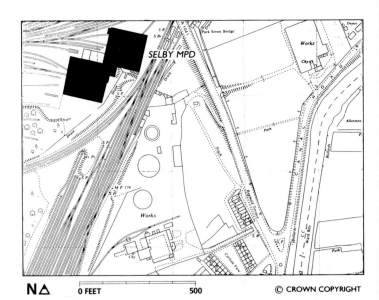

Lines of coal wagons and the abandoned **SELBY MPD** viewed from the adjacent roadway on September 29th, 1963.
WT Stubbs Collection

Map Dated: 1964
Site Location: South of the town centre, adjacent to the west side of the A1041.
Track Status: Line operational.

50D STARBECK

Location: In the fork of the Leeds and Knaresborough lines, south of Starbeck Station. (OS Map Ref: SE330557)
Directions: Cross High Street at the south end of the station and bear to the east side of the line. Continue into Spa Lane and turn right into the railway yard. A boarded crossing leads across the line to the shed.
Closed: September 13th, 1959.
Description: A brick built 2TS through road shed.
Post Closure History: Demolished. The shed floors are being excavated by the Starbeck Railway Centre preservation group. (1990)

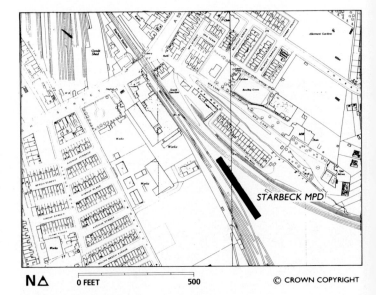

STARBECK MPD on March 20th, 1955, with ex-LNER Class J77 0–6–0T No. 68434 occupying one of the shed roads.
Dave Marriott

Map Dated: 1962 (Shed Superimposed)
Site Location: North east of Harrogate, on the south side of High Street (A59)
Track Status: Starbeck Station and line are operational.

50E SCARBOROUGH

Location: West of the Malton line, south of Scarborough Station. (OS Map Ref: TA033871)

Directions: Turn left outside of the station along Westborough, proceed along Falsgrave Road and bear left at the island along Seamer Road. The shed entrance is on the left hand side.

Closed: April 22nd, 1963

Description: Comprising of a brick built roundhouse at the north end of the yard, and a brick built 8TS dead ended shed at the south.

Post Closure History: *Demolished. Part of the site is in use as an ambulance station. (1980)*

The former 8TS shed at **SCARBOROUGH MPD** on June 2nd, 1963. Part of the depot building had, latterly, been removed leaving four of the tracks uncovered.

WT Stubbs Collection

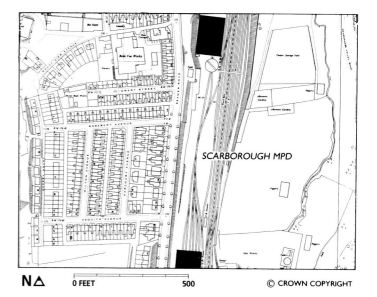

N△   0 FEET   500   © CROWN COPYRIGHT

Map Dated: 1968 (Southernmost Shed Superimposed)

Site Location: South of the town centre, adjacent to the east side of Seamer Road (A64)

Track Status: Scarborough Station and line are operational.

50F MALTON

Location: South of the line, at the west end of Malton Station. (OS Map Ref: SE785713)

Directions: A boarded crossing leads to the shed from the west end of the station.

Closed: April 22nd, 1963.

Description: A brick built 2TS through road shed.

Post Closure History: *Demolished. Site unused. (1980)*

MALTON MPD on March 8th, 1959.   *Sid Nash*

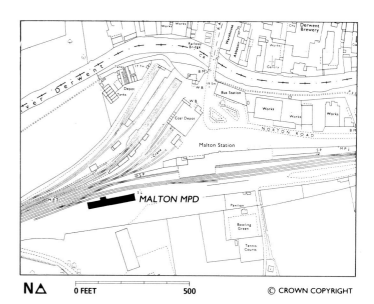

N△   0 FEET   500   © CROWN COPYRIGHT

Map Dated: 1970 (Shed Superimposed)

Site Location: South of town centre, on the south bank of the River Derwent.

Track Status: Malton Station and line are operational.

50F(s) PICKERING

Location: East of the line, south of Pickering Station. (OS Map Ref: SE796839)

Directions: Access to the shed is gained from the south side of the level crossing that takes the A170 Ripon to Scarborough Road across the line, south of the station.

Closed: April 6th, 1959.

Description: A brick built 1TS dead ended shed.

Post Closure History: Still standing and in excellent condition, in use as a timber merchants. (1990)

PICKERING MPD on August 19th, 1958, with ex-LNER Class G5 4–4–2T No. 67342 parked on the shed road.
Ken Fairey

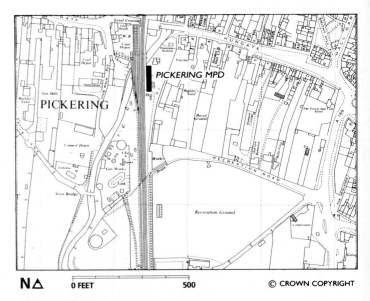

N△ 0 FEET 500 © CROWN COPYRIGHT

Map Dated: 1969

Site Location: South of the town centre.

Track Status: Pickering Station is the southern terminus of the North Yorkshire Moors Railway. All lines lifted south of the station.

50G WHITBY

Location: West of the line, south of Whitby Station. (OS Map Ref: NZ899106)

Directions: Turn left outside the station along Windsor Terrace running parallel to the railway. The shed entrance is on the left hand side just past the end of the station platforms.

Closed: April 6th, 1959.

Description: A stone built 2TS dead ended shed.

Post Closure History: Still Standing. In use as a ships' chandlers. (1990)

An LMS design mogul and ex-LNER Class A8 4–6–2T share the yard at **WHITBY MPD** on July 5th, 1955.
Ken Fairey

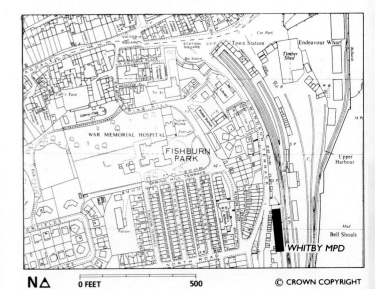

N△ 0 FEET 500 © CROWN COPYRIGHT

Map Dated: 1968

Site Location: South of the town centre, on the west bank of the River Esk.

Track Status: Whitby Station and line are operational.

51A(s) MIDDLETON IN TEESDALE

Location: On the south side of Middleton in Teesdale Station. (OS Map Ref: NY946248)

Directions: Entrance to the shed is effected from the station platform.

Closed: September 16th, 1957.

Description: A stone built 1TS dead ended shed.

Post Closure History: Demolished. The site was in use as a Caravan Park for some time.

The shed building at **MIDDLETON IN TEESDALE MPD** on July 3rd, 1960.
WT Stubbs Collection

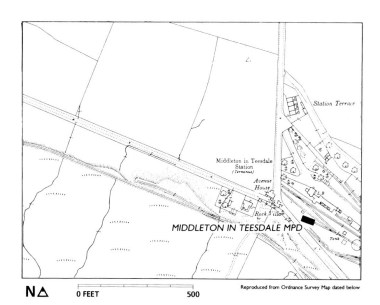

N△ 0 FEET 500 Reproduced from Ordnance Survey Map dated below

Map Dated: 1914

Site Location: South of the town centre, adjacent to the north side of the B6276.

Track Status: Middleton in Teesdale Station closed in 1964. Lines lifted.

51B NEWPORT (YORKSHIRE)

Location: North of the line between Thornaby and Middlesbrough. (OS Map Ref: NZ470192)

Directions: A cinder path, leading over a footbridge and to the shed, can be found on the north side of the A176 Middlesbrough to Thornaby Road, some 2 miles west of Middlesbrough and opposite the Greyhound Stadium.

Closed: May 31st, 1958.

Description: A building complex consisting of 2 brick built roundhouses and a 3TS dead ended shed.

Post Closure History: Demolished. The entire site is part of the Tees Marshalling Yards. (1990)

NEWPORT (YORKSHIRE) MPD on April 20th, 1958, some month or so before the locomotives transferred to the new depot at Thornaby. The site of this shed was subsequently swallowed up by expansion of the Tees Marshalling Yard.
Brian Hilton

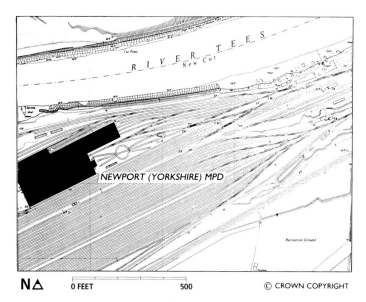

N△ 0 FEET 500 © CROWN COPYRIGHT

Map Dated: 1952

Site Location: West of Middlesbrough town centre, on the south bank of the River Tees.

Track Status: Middlesbrough Station and line are operational.

51D MIDDLESBROUGH

Location: South of the line, east of Middlesbrough Station. (OS Map Ref: NZ500204)

Directions: Turn right outside of the station into Exchange Place, first left into Marton Road, left again into Zetland Place and right into Wood Street. The shed entrance is on the left hand side.

Closed: May 31st, 1958.

Description: Originally a brick built 3 roundhouse shed, but latterly very dilapidated and one roundhouse was without any roofing.

Post Closure History: *Demolished. Site now in use as a car park. (1990)*

Ex-LNER Class Q6 0–8–0s Nos 63340 and 63373 stand outside of a portion of **MIDDLESBROUGH MPD** that was still standing in May 1954.   *Photomatic*

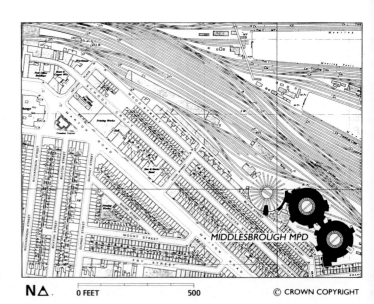

Map Dated: 1954

Site Location: East of the town centre, on the north side of Marton Road (A172)

Track Status: Middlesbrough Station and line are operational.

51D(s) GUISBOROUGH

Location: On the east side of the line, at the south end of Guisborough Station. (OS Map Ref: NZ615158)

Directions: Entrance to the shed is effected from the station platform.

Closed: September 20th, 1954.

Description: A corrugated iron 1TS dead ended shed.

Post Closure History: *Demolished.*

A general view of the station facilities and **GUISBOROUGH MPD**. The shed building can be seen just to the right of the station canopy.   *Andrew Pearson*
By courtesy of The Guisborough Museum

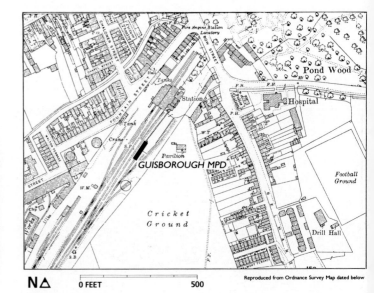

Map Dated: 1928

Site Location: South of the town centre, on the west side of Bow Street (A171)

Track Status: Guisborough Station closed in 1964. Lines lifted.

51J NORTHALLERTON

Location: Alongside of the low level goods line, on the west side of Northallerton Station. (OS Map Ref: SE363933)

Directions: Turn right outside of the station under the bridge and a cinder path leads to the shed on the right hand side by the level crossing.

Closed: March 4th, 1963

Description: A small depot complex composed of two adjoining brick built ITS sheds, one with a through road.

Post Closure History: *Demolished. Site of commercial development. (1990)*

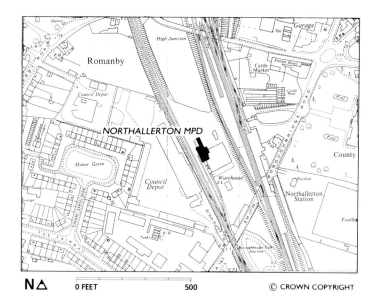

NΔ　　0 FEET　　　　500　　　　　© CROWN COPYRIGHT

Map Dated: 1969 (Shed Superimposed)
Site Location: West of the town centre, on the north side of Boroughbridge Road (A167)
Track Status: Northallerton Station and high level line are operational.

Ex-LNER Class J25 0–6–0 No. 65726 simmers in the entrance to **NORTHALLER-TON MPD** on a March day in 1954.　　*Allan Sommerfield Collection*

51J(s) LEYBURN

Location: North of the line, adjacent to Leyburn Station.(OS Map Ref: SE117903)

Directions: Entrance to the shed is effected from the station platform.

Closed: May 2nd, 1954.

Description: A stone built ITS dead ended shed.

Post Closure History: *Demolished*

Despite over ten years of closure, all the facilities were still intact at the small stone built **LEYBURN MPD** on June 1st, 1963.　　*WT Stubbs Collection*

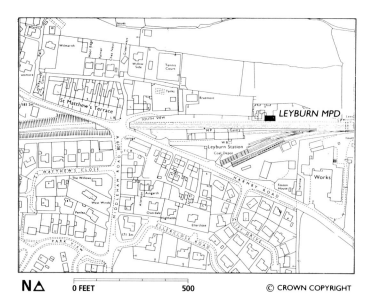

NΔ　　0 FEET　　　　500　　　　　© CROWN COPYRIGHT

Map Dated: 1981 (Shed Superimposed)
Site Location: East of the town centre, on the north side of Harmby Road (A684)
Track Status: Leyburn Station closed in 1954. Line operational.

51K SALTBURN

Location: South of the line, west of Saltburn Station. (OS Map Ref: NZ659213)

Directions: Turn right outside of the station into Dundas Street, proceed along Burton Terrace, and a cinder path leads to the shed from the right hand side.

Closed: January 28th, 1958.

Description: A brick built 2TS dead ended shed.

Post Closure History: *Demolished. Site unused. (1990)*

SALTBURN MPD in BR days.   *Kenneth L. Taylor Collection*

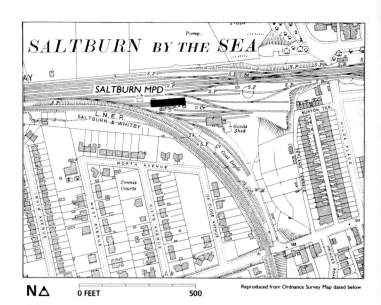

Map Dated: 1928

Site Location: North of the town centre, on the west side of Station Street.

Track Status: Saltburn Station and line are operational.

51L THORNABY

Location: North of the line, east of Thornaby Station. (OS Map Ref: NZ460185)

Directions: Turn left at the end of the station approach road into Mandale Road (A176) and fork left into the old Middlesbrough Road. The shed entrance is on the left hand side.

Closed: December 1964 (Steam)

Description: A concrete built roundhouse and 12TS through road shed

Post Closure History: *Partially Still standing. The straighthouse is in use as a Diesel Depot (Code TE).*

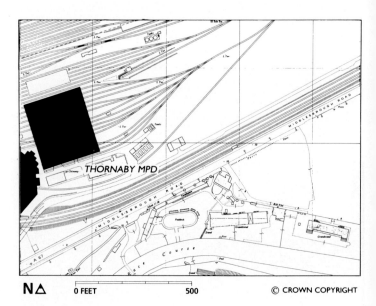

Map Dated: 1968

Site Location: West of Middlesbrough town centre, on the north side of Middlesbrough Road (A67)

Track Status: Thornaby Station and line are operational.

The roundhouse portion was used for wagon repairs for some years. Demolished in 1988.

Completed in 1958 and opened on June 5th **THORNABY MPD** represented BR's final attempt at designing and building a depot exclusively for steam locomotives use, although much of the detailed designing had been modified to allow for the imminent incursion of diesel locomotion. The depot immediately replaced the sheds at Middlesbrough and Newport (Yorkshire), and within a year had also assumed the duties of Stockton and Haverton Hill. This view, of the west end with the roundhouse building on the right hand side, shows that steam was still much in evidence on August 29th, 1961.   *Ken Fairey*

53D BRIDLINGTON

Location: East of the line, south of Bridlington Station. (OS Map Ref: TA177668)

Directions: Leave the station via the approach road, turn right into Hilderthorpe Road, right into Cardigan Road and the shed entrance is on the left hand side, just before the bridge.

Closed: December 1st, 1958.

Description: A brick built 3TS dead ended shed.

Post Closure History: *Demolished in November 1986.*

BRIDLINGTON MPD hosted visiting steam locomotives for many years after closure, particularly during the summer season, as this scene, taken on June 2nd, 1963, shows.
WT Stubbs Collection

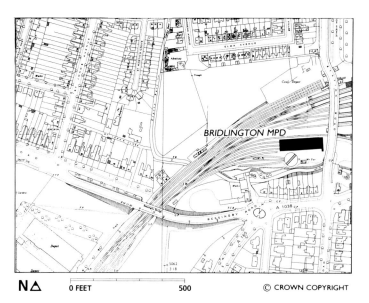

N△   0 FEET   500   © CROWN COPYRIGHT

Map Dated: 1963

Site Location: In the town centre, on the north side of Bessingby Road (A1038)

Track Status: Bridlington Station and line are operational.

53E CUDWORTH

Location: On the west side of the Cudworth to Normanton line, north of Cudworth Goods Junction. (OS Map Ref: SE377107)

Directions: Turn left outside of Royston & Notton (LMR) Station into Lund Hill Lane, left into Cross Lane and left, at the end, into Pools Lane. Turn almost immediately right into Boulder Bridge Lane, continue along the path under the railway embankment and the shed entrance is on the left hand side.

Closed: July 30th, 1951.

Description: A brick built 8TS dead ended shed.

Post Closure History: *Demolished. Site unused (1990)*

An elevated view of the ex-Hull and Barnsley depot at **CUDWORTH MPD** taken in 1947.
Allan Sommerfield Collection

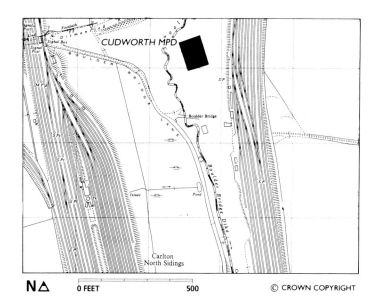

N△   0 FEET   500   © CROWN COPYRIGHT

Map Dated: 1962. (Shed superimposed)

Site Location: North of Barnsley, on the east side of the Wakefield Road (A61)

Track Status: Lines lifted.

36D BARNSLEY

Location: On the east side of Barnsley Exchange Station. (OS Map Ref: SE347065)

Directions: Turn left outside the station along the bus station. Turn left into Queens Road and the shed entrance is on the left, just past the level crossing.

Closed: January 4th, 1960.

Description: A brick built 2TS through road shed

Post Closure History: *Demolished. Part of site occupied by new Barnsley Station up platform.*

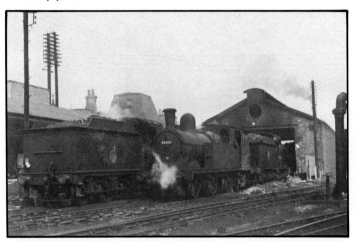

Ex-LNER Class N5 0–6–2T No. 69365 heads a line of locomotives at **BARNSLEY MPD** on March 20th, 1955. The shed area was utterly inadequate for the number of locomotives it was expected to service and as a result engines were parked on any sidings in the area that were available.   *Dave Marriott*

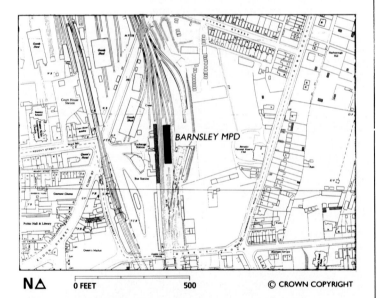

N△   0 FEET   500   © CROWN COPYRIGHT

Map Dated: 1962 (Shed superimposed)

Site Location: In the town centre, on the east side of Eldon Street (A61).

Track Status: Barnsley Station and line are operational.

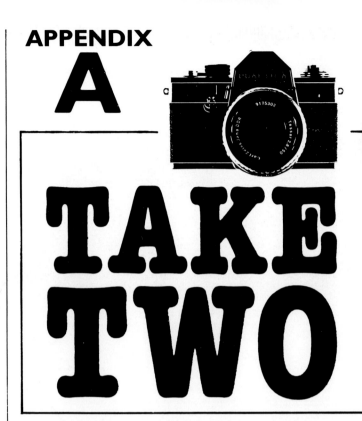

APPENDIX A
TAKE TWO

In earlier volumes space has been at a premium and squeezing everything in has been a difficulty. With the primary objective of the books to locate and identify the position of each shed, photographic content, whilst very important, has been modified to allow the publishing of a complete set of maps. Happily, because of the nature of this volume, although no smaller in content than previous issues, space is available to correct the imbalance and this Appendix is devoted to photographs that had to be omitted from *Volumes 1 and 2*.

Whilst on the subject of photographs, it may have been felt that some have been of inferior quality, or have appeared in other publications. This, however, more reflects the scarcity of shots of some sheds rather than any tardiness on my part in trying to obtain good quality unpublished originals. The larger sprawling depots had little photographic merit and were difficult to portray and those smaller depots that closed soon after 1948 were so obscure as to be almost forgotten. It is probably in the nature of things that when an abundance of riches surrounds, then the value of such diminishes. Pre-war enthusiasts in the halcyon days of steam could be forgiven for imagining that the scene would last forever and fail to appreciate the worthiness of the mundane steam depot. In fact many authorities on Engine Sheds feel that if it had not been for the efforts of WA (Bill) Camwell, much of it before the war, large numbers of sheds would have gone photographically unrecorded. Post war awareness of the impermanence of things no doubt increased the activities of the amateur photographer but whilst the taking of pictures of locomotives has always had a popular and expert following, that of specifically photographing sheds and depots has been the province of a very small band of enthusiasts, and it is to these that fellow shed book authors and myself offer some very grateful thanks.

As these particular volumes have been devoted to BR motive power depots I have striven to use contemporary views, but even this modest objective has been found to border on the impossible and many of the following photographs are of pre-nationalisation origin. Likewise, despite intense enquiries, it has proved to be impossible to accumulate photographs of all the 666 locations. Having said that only shots of the facilities at *Southampton New Docks, Wickford, Camp Hill, Washwood Heath, Water Orton and North Leith* remain elusive for one reason or another. Doubtless, views of these sheds are in existence. Those of us at the Engine Shed Society would be keen to see them.

82C(s) ANDOVER   48

The former GW depot at **ANDOVER MPD** in June 1954. Both the GWR and SR had separate sheds on the same site and both retained their identity throughout their existence.   *Photomatic*

71G BATH GREEN PARK   22

BR Standard Class 5MT 4–6–0 No. 73054 standing outside of the former S&DJR 4TS wooden structure at **BATH GREEN PARK MPD** on September 1st, 1961.
WT Stubbs Collection

83B(s) BARNSTAPLE   37

GWR Class 4300 2–6–0 No. 6343 standing outside of **BARNSTAPLE MPD** on June 10th, 1935.   *Allan Sommerfield Collection*

82A(s) BATH SPA   22

Ex-GWR Class 4500 2–6–2T No. 5528, still in its pre-BR livery, standing in the entrance to **BATH SPA MPD** in 1949. This depot, with its arrangement of water tank supported on cast iron columns forming the roof, was similar in design to the one at Glyn Neath MPD *(See Volume 2, P.73).*   *Allan Sommerfield Collection*

81D(s) BASINGSTOKE GWR   47

A pre-war view of **BASINGSTOKE GWR MPD**. In like fashion with the two depots at Salisbury, this shed closed in 1950 and all activity transferred to the former SR building at the opposite end of the station.   *Bernard Matthews Collection*

83B(s) BRIDGWATER   23

BRIDGWATER MPD in pre-war days. When the adjacent Carriage Workshops buildings were rationalised, isolating the shed building, a new roof was constructed out of corrugated asbestos in single pitch style.   *Allan Sommerfield Collection*

BRISTOL BARROW ROAD MPD in LMS days. *Bernard Matthews Collection*

CANTERBURY WEST MPD in 1926. The locomotive in the yard, ex-SE&CR Class R 0–6–0 No. A126, was fitted with cut-down boiler mountings for working the Canterbury & Whitstable line. *Bernard Matthews Collection*

A general view of **BRISTOL BATH ROAD MPD** on July 9th, 1960. *Hugh Ballantyne*

CHESHAM MPD on August 4th, 1959. The facilities included a water tower, water column and, visible just to the right of the main signal, an engine pit. *Alan A. Jackson*

Prime ex-LMS motive power line up at **CAMDEN MPD** on July 20th, 1958. *Brian Hilton*

Ex-GWR Class 5700 0–6–0PT No. 3746 standing in the shed yard at **CHIPPENHAM MPD** on September 18th, 1960. *Allan Sommerfield Collection*

DEVONS ROAD MPD in pre-dieselisation days on September 16th, 1950.
Brian Hilton

EWER STREET MPD viewed from a passing diverted Woolwich to Cannon Street train on October 1st, 1960. *AE Bennett*

DORCHESTER MPD plays host to a mixed bag of ex-SR locomotives, including ex-L&SWR Class T9 4–4–0 No. 30119 sporting a tender number in SR style. The view was taken in May 1952. *Chris Bush Collection*

HAMWORTHY JUNCTION MPD in 1937. *WA Camwell*

Hopelessly inadequate for the servicing of the large numbers of locomotives that a commuter line requires as an operational necessity, **ENFIELD TOWN MPD** occupied a cramped site on the west side of the station. Ex-LNER Class N7/1 0–6–2T No. 69670 heads a line of locomotives in the shed yard, awaiting their next duties, on July 13th, 1958. *Ken Fairey*

Ex-LNER Class N2/2 0–6–2T No. 69531, complete with condensing apparatus, simmering in the shed yard at **HATFIELD MPD** on April 24th, 1960. *Ken Fairey*

HITCHIN MPD was almost an integral part of the station buildings. This view, from the adjacent station platform, shows BR built Class L1 2–6–4T No. 67746 standing outside of the shed building on March 13th, 1957. *WT Stubbs Collection*

Former SR Class E1 0–6–0T No. 3 *RYDE* standing outside of **NEWPORT (IOW) MPD** on June 17th, 1956. *Ken Fairey*

The facilities in early BR days at **LAMBOURN MPD**. The foundations to the former shed are visible, midway between the platform edge and the Goods Shed, with the engine pit immediately in front of the site. *Joe Moss*

Ex-LMS Class 8F 2–8–0 No. 48459, Ex-GWR Class 5100 2–6–2T Nos. 5158, 4105, 5164 and County Class 4–6–0 No. 1016 *COUNTY OF HANTS* line up outside of **NEWTON ABBOT MPD** in June 1960. *Chris Bush Collection*

NEWBURY MPD was just a couple of tracks adjacent to the Lambourn Branch bay platform. This view shows the stand siding and water column in BR days. *Lens of Sutton*

The compact layout of **PALACE GATES MPD** in LNER days, complete with adjacent allotments and meticulously constructed coal stacks. *WA Camwell*

RAMSGATE MPD in the last year of steam operation, with West Country Class 4–6–2 No. 34012 *LAUNCESTON*, Class V 4–4–0s Nos. 30919 *HARROW* and 30921 *SHREWSBURY*, and West Country Class 4–6–2s Nos 34027 *TAW VALLEY* and 34001 *EXETER* standing in the shed yard on March 15th, 1959.   *Hugh Ballantyne*

SALISBURY MPD was re-roofed in the 1950s and this view taken on September 30th, 1961 shows the shed buildings in their final form.   *WT Stubbs Collection*

The abandoned shed buildings at **ST.PHILIPS MARSH MPD** in June 1964.
AG Ellis Collection

A 1959 view as ex-SR Class C14 0–4–0T No. 30588, the Southampton Town Quay branch engine, shares the stabling area at **SOUTHAMPTON TERMINUS MPD** with a sundry collection of former GW locomotives, whilst in the background an ex-SR Class T9 4–4–0 utilises the turntable.   *Peter Hay*

SALISBURY GWR MPD on September 18th, 1938. The depot did not last too long after nationalisation, the opportunity being taken in 1950 to concentrate locomotive servicing at the adjacent ex-SR depot.   *Bernard Matthews Collection*

Despite being in the middle of a bustling metropolis, the site of **SPITALFIELDS MPD**, as with EWER STREET MPD, is today virtually inaccessible with both occupying elevated positions, well above street level, and surrounded by busy electrified lines. This view, in LNER times, captures a rare quiet moment with a couple of ex-GE Class J68 0–6–0Ts on the shed road.   *WA Camwell*

A post war view of the wooden built ITS **STAINES MPD**.
Allan Sommerfield Collection

The 12TS 'Jubilee Shed' at **STRATFORD MPD** in LNER days.
Chris Bush Collection

A vintage view of the cramped roundhouse at **TAUNTON MPD**.
Allan Sommerfield Collection

The wooden shed at **TEMPLECOMBE MPD** was in a pretty awful condition when viewed in early BR days on August 26th, 1950. Less than a year later it was totally rebuilt in brick and, by now being part of the Southern Region, in the style developed by the Southern Railway and employed at such locations as Tonbridge and Redhill.
Peter Winding

The small wooden shed at **TEMPLECOMBE UPPER MPD**, playing host to most of ex-LSWR Class K10 4–4–0 No. 145, in SR days.
WA Camwell

A fine view of **WATFORD JUNCTION MPD** on March 8th, 1964, showing the two patterns of roof with which it existed throughout its BR days. The easternmost section had been re-roofed by the LMS, whilst the other portion retained its original L&NWR design.
Ken Fairey

The disused facility at **WATLINGTON MPD** in September 1958.   *Photomatic*

BR Class 2MT 2–6–0 No. 78063 standing in front of the 12TS building at **WILLES-DEN MPD** on February 21st, 1965.   *Ken Fairey*

An LMS design Mogul standing inside the partially roofless shed building at **WELLS GWR MPD** on September 1st, 1961.   *WT Stubbs Collection*

A delightfully rustic scene at **YATTON MPD** in February 1949, with a chicken run sandwiched between the stone built shed building and the running line.   *John Edgington*

The stone built shed at **WELLS LMS MPD**, complete with *ad hoc* roofing arrangement, just before nationalisation.   *Bernard Matthews Collection*

The former SR shed buildings at **YEOVIL TOWN MPD** on July 11th, 1957, with ex-SR West Country Class 4–6–2 No. 34024 *TAMAR VALLEY* simmering alongside the coal stage.   *John Edgington*

30A(s) BRENTWOOD 8

A general view of **BRENTWOOD MPD** on August 7th, 1939, with LNER Class D16 4–4–0 No. 8856 (Later BR No. 62547) calling at the station and fellow class member No. 8782 (Later BR No. 62613) standing in the shed yard. *WA Camwell*

30A(s) EPPING 8

Ex-GN Class C12 4–4–2T No. 67363 standing outside of the shed building at **EPPING MPD** during August 1953. After nationalisation Epping became the responsibility of the London Transport Executive and was rebuilt by them in 1949. *Photomatic*

89A(s) LLANIDLOES 93

LMS design Class 2MT 2–6–0 No. 46502 standing in the shed entrance at **LLANID-LOES MPD** *WT Stubbs Collection*

32B(s) FELIXSTOWE 27

Even in LNER days **FELIXSTOWE BEACH MPD** was of little substance, with just a back wall remaining when viewed on April 17th, 1938. *Bernard Matthews Collection*

FELIXSTOWE TOWN 27

The other facility, although of an 'unofficial' nature was at FELIXSTOWE TOWN, and this view, taken on August 31st, 1960, shows engine pits on both sides of the main line. By this time both the spurs and pits were out of use. *WT Stubbs Collection*

89A(s) LLANFYLLIN 93

The small wooden built **LLANFYLLIN MPD** in GWR days. *WA Camwell*

Ex-GWR Class 2251 0–6–0 No. 2204 and BR Class 2 2–6–0 No. 78005 share the accomodation at **PORTMADOC MPD** on September 11th, 1960.
WT Stubbs Collection

The proximity of **WALTON ON NAZE MPD** to the station is clearly illustrated in this pre-war photograph. LNER Class F3 2–4–2T No. 8060 stands on the turntable road on March 28th, 1937.
WA Camwell

An Ipswich to Stowmarket DMU passing **STOWMARKET MPD** in September 1975. The office can be seen, behind the wagons, with the stabling road immediately in front. It was during this year that the facility was totally abandoned. *Roger Smith*

The abandoned shed at **WELLS ON SEA MPD** playing host to a rake of goods vans on August 29th, 1960.
WT Stubbs Collection

LNER Class F3 2–4–2T No. 8085 standing alongside the water column at **SWAFFHAM MPD** on August 6th, 1939.
WA Camwell

An ex-GWR Class 2200 0–6–0 locomotive standing on the former site of **WELSHPOOL MPD** on May 21st, 1961. By BR days visiting locomotives just used the engine pit facility
Roger Griffiths Collection

INDEX